IMAGES
of America

THE COLLEGE OF

PHYSICIANS OF
PHILADELPHIA

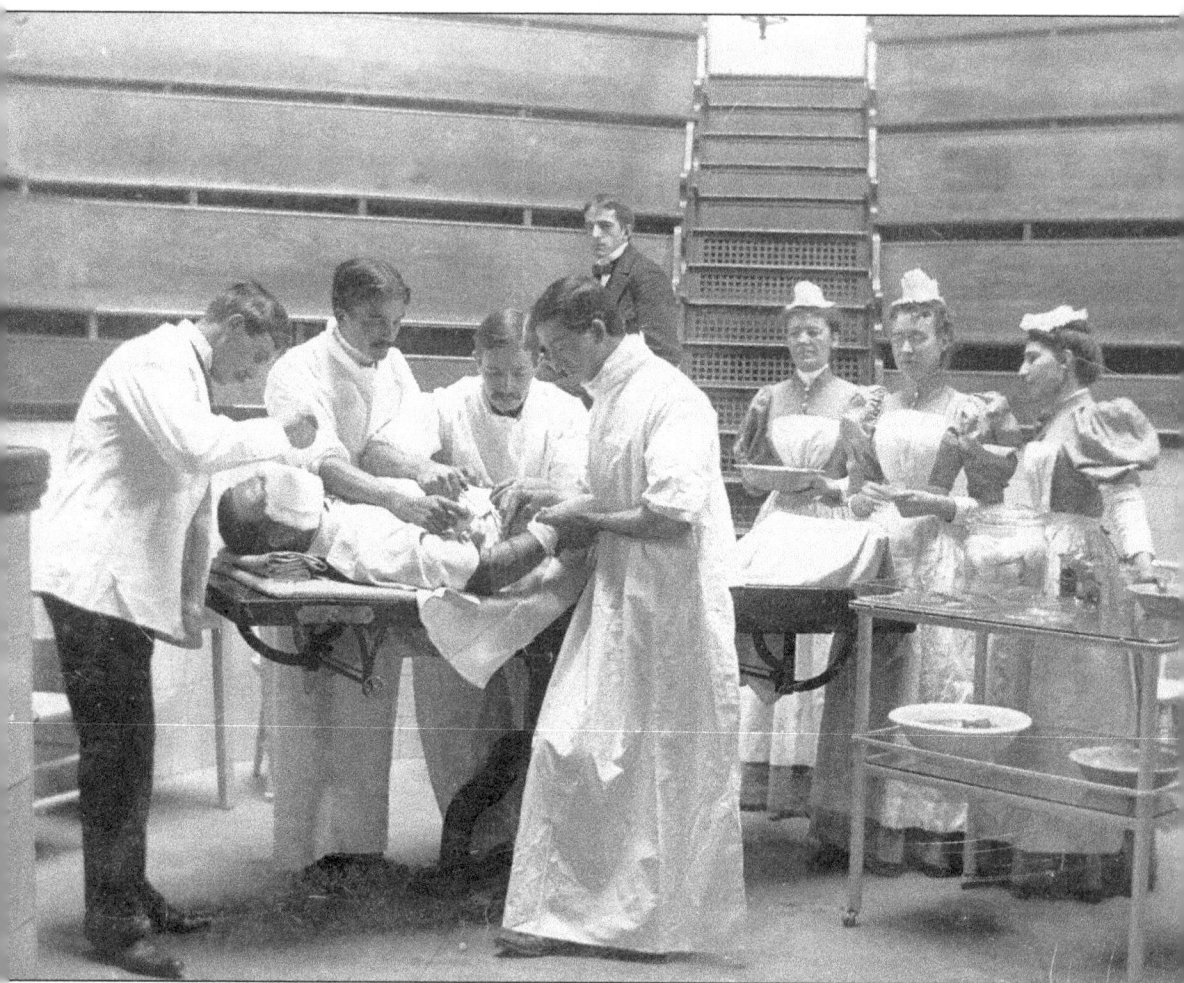

ON THE COVER: Chloroform was recognized as an anesthetic in 1847. Physicians throughout Europe and the United States soon began to use it before surgery, but many patients died on the operating table under its influence. Not until 1911 did physicians realize that chloroform sometimes affects the heart's rhythm. Surgeons gradually eliminated it during the first half of the 20th century. As this c. 1890 image shows, chloroform was administered by covering the patient's nose and mouth with a soaked gauze pad. (Courtesy of The College of Physicians of Philadelphia.)

IMAGES
of *America*

THE COLLEGE OF
PHYSICIANS OF
PHILADELPHIA

The College of Physicians of Philadelphia
Foreword by George M. Wohlreich, MD

ARCADIA
PUBLISHING

Published by Arcadia Publishing
Charleston, South Carolina

Library of Congress Control Number: 2011941252

For all general information, please contact Arcadia Publishing:
Telephone 843-853-2070
Fax 843-853-0044
E-mail sales@arcadiapublishing.com
For customer service and orders:
Toll-Free 1-888-313-2665

Visit us on the Internet at www.arcadiapublishing.com

*To the fellows of The College of Physicians of
Philadelphia—past, present, and future*

CONTENTS

FOREWORD

Walking into The College of Physicians of Philadelphia always reminds me why I went into medicine: to see—be overwhelmed by—and experience the great commonality of all our lives and all our suffering, to understand the significant advances that have occurred, and to take part in that history's future. These experiences inspire me. To learn about the journey that medicine has taken over time is to be exhilarated, challenged, and humbled.

In these pages, Kathleen Sands has compiled a wonderfully engaging pictorial digest of "The Birthplace of American Medicine."SM With a deft touch, she has selected from the college's vast archives, photographs, and written accounts that highlight the history of the college, its early leaders and practitioners, and its part in the evolution of American medicine. Sands's selection of photographs—fascinating, sometimes disturbing—underscores her narrative and documents afflictions, preserved anatomical specimens, casts, artifacts, medical instruments and procedures, operating theatres, and early teaching and research facilities. Photographs from both the Mütter Museum and the Historical Medical Library are abundantly represented.

Why should you be interested in this book? Because the college represents the common ground where medicine, health, and community merge, where the best of our past illuminates the possibilities for our future, where what makes us all too human is clearly shown.

This is not a book about specimens or famous historical figures. It is a pictorial depiction of us and our humanity.

—George M. Wohlreich, MD, FCPP
Director and Chief Executive Officer
The Thomas W. Langfitt Chair
The College of Physicians of Philadelphia

ACKNOWLEDGMENTS

This project was accomplished with the assistance of several staff members of The College of Physicians of Philadelphia. Annie Brogan, Anna Dhody, Evi Numen, and J. Nathan Bazzel answered numerous questions about the esoterica of the college. Evi also did much of the imaging work for the book, along with volunteer Jamie See. Robert D. Hicks, PhD, commented on the draft text and arranged the internship that made this project possible.

Arcadia Publishing's acquisitions editors Erin Vosgien, Darcy Mahan, and Abby Henry made the process run very smoothly.

Special thanks go to six fellows of The College of Physicians of Philadelphia. George M. Wohlreich, MD, FCPP, supplied the foreword and commented on the draft text. Andrea Baldeck, MD, FCPP, kindly permitted the inclusion of some of her beautiful photographs in the book. Four fellows generously volunteered their time to read the draft text with an eye to improving its accuracy and presentation: Bonnie B. Dorwart, MD, FCPP; Thomas Fekete, MD, FCPP; Bennett Lorber, MD, FCPP; and Kenneth J. Weiss, MD, FCPP.

And special thanks also go to the John B. Hurford '60 Humanities Center of Haverford College for dedicating a summer internship to this project. The intern was Elinor G. Hickey, who researched more than two centuries of institutional history as well as the history of medical science. She investigated hundreds of archives of photographs, medical illustrations, advertisements, pamphlets, catalogs, scrapbooks, academic notebooks, and other items held by the college. She electronically scanned relevant images and documents, photographed artifacts, and researched and wrote some of the text. This book is significantly better (and was completed significantly faster) because of Elinor's work.

As my gift to The College of Physicians of Philadelphia, I donated 1,000+ hours to research, write, and edit this book. I also donated the authorship, copyright, and royalties. I hope the collective labor of all of us who worked on this book will benefit the college through an increased public awareness of the significance of "The Birthplace of American Medicine."[SM]

—Kathleen R. Sands, PhD
Project Director

KEY TO ABBREVIATIONS USED IN THE TEXT

FCPP indicates a fellow (elected member) of The College of Physicians of Philadelphia. AB indicates a photograph taken by and used with the permission of Andrea Baldeck, MD, FCPP. All other photographs appear courtesy of The College of Physicians of Philadelphia.

INTRODUCTION

The American Revolution was nearly lost because of a terrible disease: smallpox.

The British military forces were largely immune. Since smallpox had spread throughout Europe for centuries, most of the British soldiers had already suffered mild cases of smallpox, and they were immune for life. Others had been vaccinated ("variolated"), a practice used in Britain since the 1720s.

The American natives and colonists, however, had no such immunity—and the British knew it. The natives who besieged the fort at Detroit under the direction of the Ottawa leader Pontiac on May 29, 1763, were excellent warriors, but they had never had smallpox and were therefore not immune to it. Letters exchanged between the fort's relief commander, Col. Henry Bouquet, and the British commander in chief, Sir Jeffrey Amherst, show that British military authorities discussed, sanctioned, and paid for the distribution of smallpox-infected blankets to the natives. Amherst wrote to Bouquet, "Could it not be contrived to send the smallpox among those disaffected tribes of Indians?" Bouquet responded, "I will try to inoculate the Indians by means of blankets that may fall in their hands." The following week, Amherst confirmed the plan: "You will do well to inoculate the Indians by means of blankets." And the plan worked: Multiple reports confirm that smallpox infected and killed Ottawas and their allies for years.

Twelve years later, Americans again lost a fight because of smallpox. During the Battle of Quebec in 1775, more than half of the 10,000 colonial troops contracted the disease. Their commander, Maj. Gen. John Thomas, had prohibited the vaccination of the soldiers, and he was among those who died of the disease. Some of the troops believed that the epidemic had been engineered by the British, who may have dispatched young smallpox-infected women from Quebec to defeat the colonial invasion. Whether the infection was intentional or not, it guaranteed the British victory. John Adams wrote, "Our misfortunes in Canada are enough to melt the heart of stone. The smallpox is ten times more terrible than the British, Canadians, and Indians together. This was the cause of our precipitate retreat from Quebec."

One of the officers who survived the Battle of Quebec was Gen. George Washington. He was immune, having contracted and survived smallpox many years earlier. And when he became commander in chief of the Continental Army in 1775, he issued two important orders: First, that any soldier who exhibited "the smallest sign of smallpox" was to be isolated without delay; second, that every colonial soldier who had not already had smallpox be vaccinated immediately.

These actions proved pivotal to the revolutionary cause. Washington's orders allowed the Continental Army to regain enough strength to triumph over the British forces in the battles that finally led to the decisive American victory at Yorktown in 1781.

Meanwhile, the new national government was being hammered into shape in Philadelphia—"the Athens of America," the largest city on the continent, the second largest city in the British Empire, the first capital city of the new United States, the site of the First and Second Continental Congresses, and the site of the signing of the Declaration of Independence.

But what about that smallpox?

Well, while Philadelphia was creating political history, it was also creating medical history. The nation's first medical school, first hospital, first school of anatomy, first children's hospital, first free medical clinic, first college of pharmacy, first manual of military surgery, first medical textbook, first surgical operating theater, and first women's medical college—yes, all these were also born in Philadelphia.

And the nation's first professional medical society?

Read on.

One

MEDICAL CHALLENGES IN THE NEW UNITED STATES

After Benjamin Rush (1745–1813) signed the Declaration of Independence in 1776, he envisioned an organization that would "advance the science of medicine and thereby lessen human misery." Together with 23 other physicians, Rush founded The College of Physicians of Philadelphia in 1787. This portrait of Rush by Adele von Helmbold is a copy of the original by Thomas Sully.

In his medical practice, Rush used bloodletting, a practice that had been common for centuries. After he made shallow incisions in the skin of his patient, he might place small glass cups over the wounds to create a vacuum to encourage the flow of blood. Or he might open a vein and collect the blood in a specialized bowl. Bloodletting could involve the removal of up to four pints of blood in a single treatment, sometimes causing the patient to faint. It is now known that this treatment sedated the patient but had no curative value and opened the body to infection. The practice of bloodletting stopped during the 19th century after decades of vehement argument among physicians about its effectiveness. Rush, an ardent proponent of bloodletting, resigned from the college in protest when his colleagues refused to support his position. (AB cupping and bleeding bowl.)

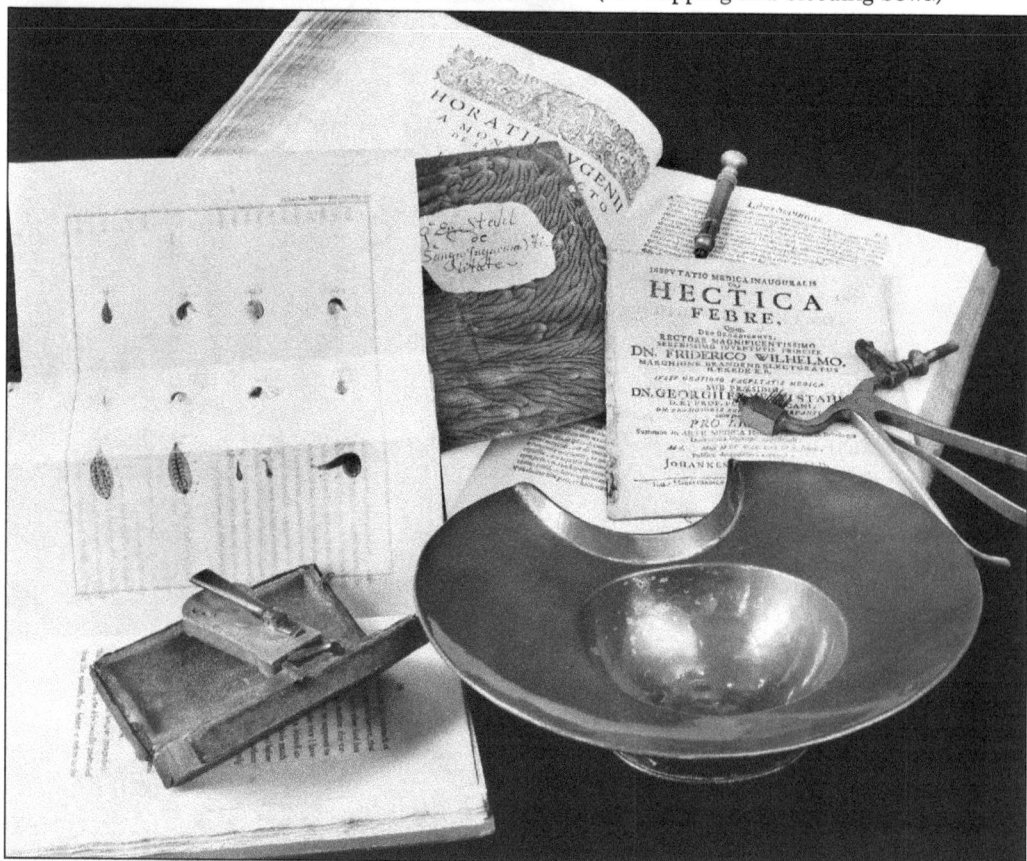

Obstetricians were the first physicians to use chloroform widely. After Queen Victoria used it in preparation for her final two childbirths, European and American women quickly accepted the practice. Another early use for chloroform was in anesthetizing wounded soldiers requiring battlefield surgery. Military surgeons used it during the Mexican-American War (1846–1848) and the American Civil War (1861–1865). (AB chloroform texts and apparatus.)

Although microscopes were developed in the late 16th century, not until the 19th century was their medical value realized. Their magnifying lenses revealed the existence of bacteria, thus laying the groundwork for the understanding of the role of germs in disease. Gradually, the wooden surfaces in medical environments (such as this early laboratory) were replaced by metal surfaces, which could be sterilized.

During the 18th and 19th centuries, courts often institutionalized people for alcoholism, depression, epilepsy, and other conditions that are now referred to physicians rather than to judges. The Blockley Almshouse, commonly called "Old Blockley" and later known as Philadelphia General Hospital, provided the first government-sponsored care of the poor in the United States. It included a hospital, a workhouse, an orphanage, and an insane asylum. These images show women from the insane asylum and men from the workhouse. Most of the residents paid for their room and board by doing manual labor around Old Blockley.

Yellow fever created some of the worst epidemics in the early United States. The disease takes its name from the jaundice that accompanies liver damage. Internal bleeding occurs in the stomach and intestines, with the blood becoming black and grainy through partial digestion. In the final phase of the disease, the patient may vomit this partly digested blood. This illustration from the 1780s shows this dreaded final stage.

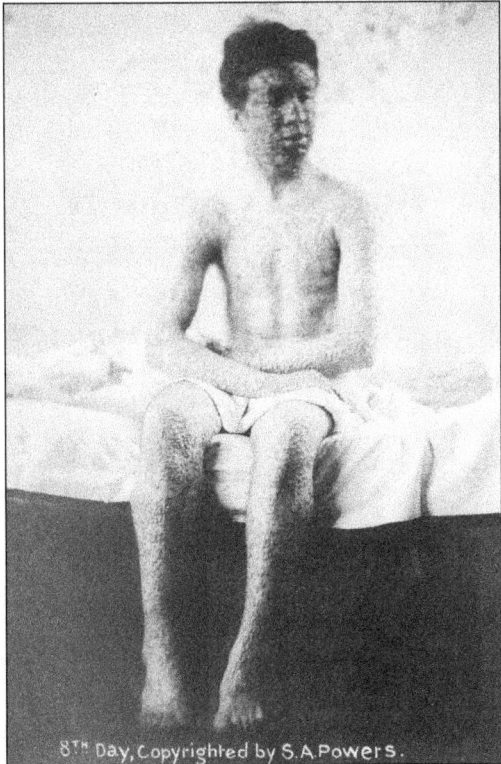

8TH Day, Copyrighted by S.A.Powers.

Even more terrible than yellow fever was smallpox, the deadliest disease in the history of humankind. During the 18th century, smallpox epidemics spread wildly across North America, devastating urban populations along the Atlantic seaboard, all throughout the South, deep into Texas and Mexico, and as far north as Canada and Alaska. One of medical science's greatest triumphs was the elimination of this scourge from the Earth in 1979.

Until major social reforms produced improvements in water purification and sewage disposal, millions of Americans died each year from waterborne diseases such as dysentery, typhoid, and poliomyelitis. Filthy public toilets such as this one were a major part of the problem. Physicians had to fight these diseases without understanding the fecal–oral method of disease transmission.

CHOLERA.

THE COMMON
Bowel Complaint,

Called a Diarrhea, very generally exists from one to ten or more days before an attack of Cholera. Have this Bowel Complaint cured, and you thereby prevent the *existence* and *growth* of this destructive Cholera.

The first stage of
CHOLERA is Curable.

It is a watery discharge from the bowels, like rice or barley water, or whey, with loss of bodily strength, &c. Do not neglect these symptoms. Send immediately for medical aid. Go to bed and be covered with blankets; have a mustard plaster put to the pit of the stomach; have dry hot oats in flannel bags, as soon as possible, placed on the bowels, to the small of the back, the feet, and elsewhere about the body. These means *timely* used will produce a profuse sweating, stop the watery discharges from the bowels, and *keep off the cold, blue, and too fatal collapse*, and enable your Physician to be instrumental *in saving your life.*

THREE FACTS
SHOULD BE GENERALLY KNOWN.

1st. A neglected Bowel Complaint (or *looseness of bowels,* often called *lax* or *flux,* and by the Physicians *diarrhea*), is followed by the Cholera.

2d. A profuse and continued sweating in bed by means of dry heat applied to the body will arrest the tendency to the fatal collapse.

3d. Ignorance and a want of previous preparation have, in a very great measure, caused the deaths from Cholera.

A PHYSICIAN'S ADVICE.

P.S. Have in your house, at hand, mustard, several flannel bags which will hold from one to two gallons, a quantity of oats, and conveniencies for *quickly* heating the oats.

August 20, 1832.

This 1832 broadside is a reminder that cholera was one of most dangerous of the waterborne diseases, killing tens of millions of people worldwide during the 19th century. Cholera can cause death within mere hours after the onset of symptoms: diarrhea, rapid pulse, vomiting, and shock.

Pulmonary tuberculosis (also called TB and consumption) killed huge numbers of the urban American population during the 19th century. Humans have suffered from this disease for at least 6,000 years, and TB has been in the Americas for over 2,000. Many famous Americans died of tuberculosis, including Henry David Thoreau, Stephen Crane, Thomas Wolfe, Stephen Foster, James Monroe, Eleanor Roosevelt, Alexander Graham Bell, W.C. Fields, Jay Gould, and Paul Laurence Dunbar. In the late 19th and early 20th centuries, the most common treatment in the United States was isolation in a sanatorium. Some of the rooms in the Pine Ridge Camp for Consumptives in Foster, Rhode Island, here photographed about 1930, were converted trolley cars, their elevation from the ground increasing the light and air available to the patient. The location of this sanatorium in a cold climate was part of the therapy: The diseased lungs were believed to breathe more easily in "bracing" air than in warm air.

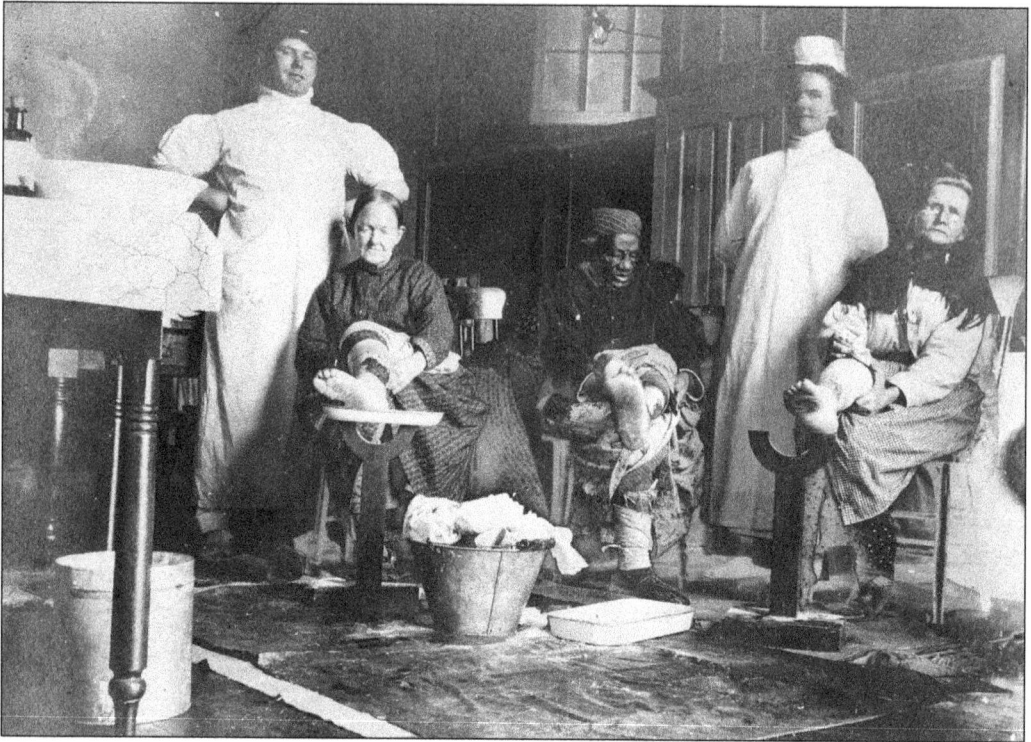

Chronic sores of the foot and leg were very common during the 18th and 19th centuries. These sores were caused by many underlying medical problems, such as heart disease, nerve damage, obstruction of the lymph glands, and trauma. These images show patients of the Old Blockley leg ward and a stereoscopic photograph of a foot cancer. Stereoscopic photography assisted medical education by making the images seem more realistic. When medical students looked at two side-by-side stereoscopic photographs of this diseased foot through a specialized viewer, they were able to get an approximate sense of how far the cancer had penetrated the flesh.

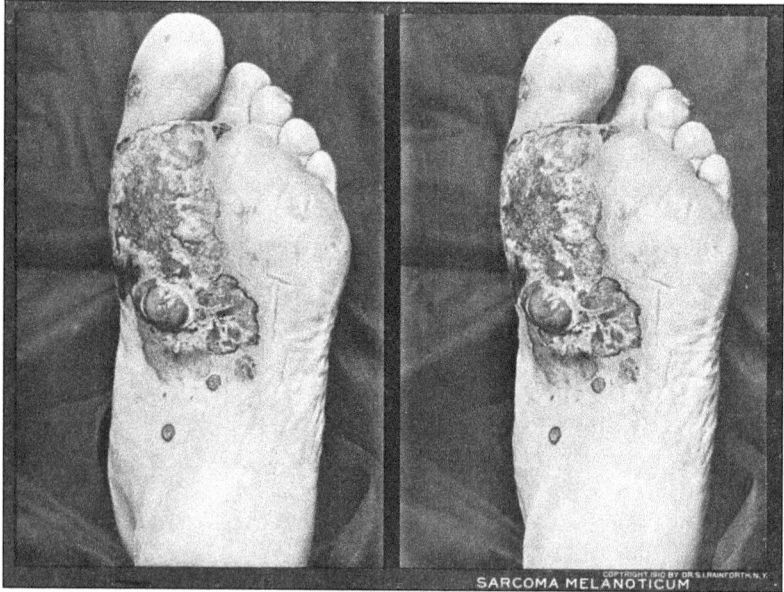

SARCOMA MELANOTICUM

Hansen's disease (formerly called leprosy) is a chronic bacterial disease that has afflicted people for at least 4,000 years. Contrary to popular belief, this disease does not cause body parts to fall off, but nerve damage coupled with infection sometimes creates a need for amputation. The disease is transmitted though the air during prolonged close contact with an infected person. Most of the world's population is naturally immune. (AB.)

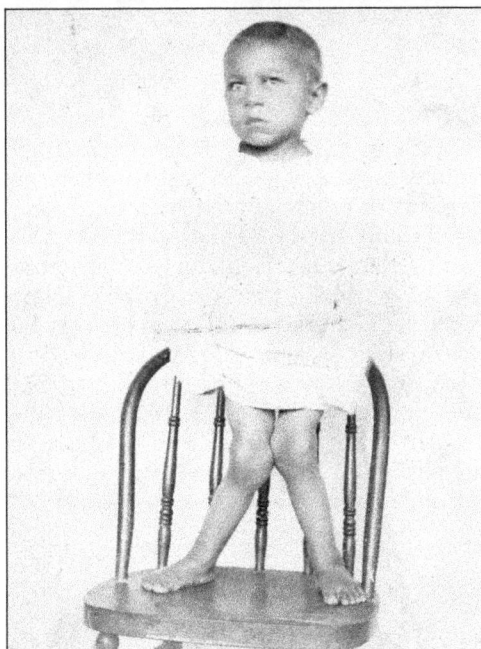

Uncorrected birth defects and childhood deformities occurred frequently in the 18th and 19th centuries. This child is afflicted with *genu valgum* (knock knee). Although this defect usually corrects itself over time, it sometimes requires leg braces or surgery. Other childhood deformities of the leg bones include *genu varum* (bow legs), which can result from deficiencies in vitamin D and calcium, and *genu recurvatum*, in which the knee bends backward.

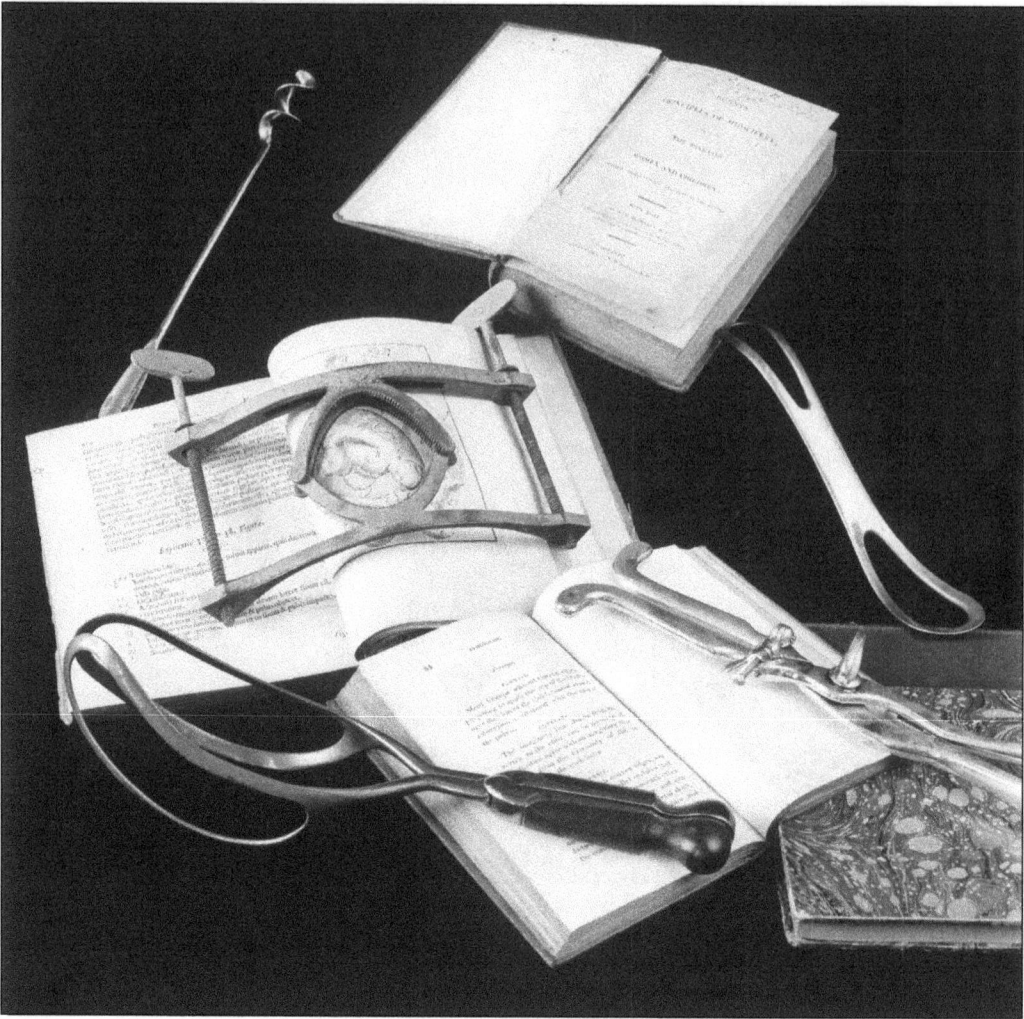

Humans are the only mammals that routinely need help giving birth. The ability to walk upright requires human legs to be close together, thus narrowing the pelvic opening. Also, the relatively large brains of humans require large skulls, which pass through the birth canal with difficulty. Until the 18th century, those who assisted women in labor were other women called midwives. During that century, male physicians began to replace female midwives as assistants during childbirth. At this time, doctors had no knowledge of bacteria and did not routinely wash their hands before and after tending to patients. Puerperal fever, a potentially deadly bacterial infection, was regularly transmitted to patients by doctors. When Oliver Wendell Holmes, MD, published *The Contagiousness of Puerperal Fever* (1843) and advised regular hand-washing as a means to prevent infection, other physicians scornfully rejected this recommendation. One said, "Doctors are gentlemen, and gentlemen's hands are always clean." Today, of course, both men and women are physicians and midwives, and all disinfect their hands regularly. (AB apparatus and texts relating to midwifery.)

Lack of antiseptic birthing procedures contributed to a high mortality rate among women and infants. Agnes, Agatha, Adelaide, and Aloysia Newton were born on February 12, 1890. The birth of quadruplets in the 19th century was unusual, of course, and the survival of all four infants plus the mother was extremely rare.

Infantile Paralysis.
After Operation with apparatus

Polio (also called poliomyelitis or infantile paralysis) was one of the most feared childhood diseases of the 20th century. Caused by a virus, it was documented for hundreds of years before it began to spread rapidly throughout Europe and the United States. Vaccines developed in the 1950s reduced the number of cases from hundreds of thousands per year to none. In 1994, the Americas were declared free of polio.

Yellow fever, smallpox, cholera, tuberculosis, and polio were just a few of the challenges for physicians in the 18th and 19th centuries. Assisting Benjamin Rush in founding The College of Physicians of Philadelphia was John Morgan (1735–1789), a founder of the first medical school in North America in 1765 at The College of Philadelphia (later called the University of Pennsylvania). This portrait of Morgan is by Isaac Eugene Craig (1830–after 1878), a copy of the original by the great neoclassical painter Angelica Kauffman (1741–1807).

Another of the founders of The College of Physicians of Philadelphia was Adam Kuhn (1741–1817), physician to the family of George Washington. Admired by Rush as Philadelphia's leading physician during the last quarter of the 18th century, Kuhn was president of the college from 1808 until his death. This portrait of Kuhn was painted by Louis Hasselbusch (1863–1938).

Also a founder was John Redman (1722–1808), who served as the college's president from its inception in 1787 until 1805. With his superlative education, Redman trained many of Philadelphia's leading physicians, including Morgan, Shippen, and Rush. This unsigned and undated miniature drawing of Redman in crayon, chalk, and pencil was probably drawn by a traveling French portraitist in the 1790s.

Another founder was William Shippen Jr. (1736–1808), director of hospitals for the Continental Army during the American Revolution. The first lecturer in anatomy in the new country of the United States, Shippen followed Redman as president of The College of Physicians of Philadelphia, serving from 1805 to 1808. This portrait was painted by an unidentified copyist (possibly Rembrandt Peale, 1788–1860) after the original by Gilbert Stuart (1755–1828).

Rush, Morgan, Kuhn, Redman, Shippen, and the 19 other physicians who founded The College of Physicians of Philadelphia agreed that the college's motto would be *Non Sibi Sed Toti* ("Not For Oneself But For All"). Here is the motto on the seal created in 1787 by Robert Scott (or Scot), the first chief engraver of the US Mint and designer of the first coins struck by the new government of the United States of America. The new institution would be both a college and a professional society. As a college, it would discuss matters of public interest, develop professional standards, and encourage collegial relations among like-minded people. As a professional society, it would provide a way for fellows (elected members) to research medical issues in a professional library and to learn from colleagues through meetings and lectures.

Two

HOUSING THE COLLEGE

The College of Physicians of Philadelphia initially met in borrowed or rented quarters. The first building owned by the college was on Locust Street and the second on South Twenty-second Street. Both resulted from the determination of Silas Weir Mitchell (1829–1914), MD, FCPP, who spent a great part of his life insuring a permanent home for the college. This portrait of Mitchell is by Franz Dvorak (1862–1927).

Thomas Dent Mütter's donation of his collection of pathological specimens to the college created a need for a building owned by the college. Mütter required the college to construct a fireproof building to house his collection. The Locust Street building was designed by Philadelphia architect James H. Windrim (1840–1919), whose later masterpiece, the Grand Lodge of Philadelphia, would be called by many people "the wonder of the Masonic world." Completed in 1863, the Locust Street building served as home to The College of Physicians of Philadelphia until 1909.

The opening of the Locust Street building created more access to library and museum resources for the members of the college. It also increased the college's visibility within the medical and scientific communities, becoming the meeting place for several other societies whose rental fees added to the college's income. "Conversation meetings" among like-minded professional men kept the building open long into the evenings. After the end of the Civil War, the college's membership expanded and donations increased. In addition to new library and museum acquisitions, the college accumulated significant collections of fine art, decorative art, and furniture. Even with the addition of a third story in 1885, the college outgrew the Locust Street building before the turn of the century.

The prestigious architectural firm of Walter Cope (1860–1902) and John Stewardson (1858–1896) designed the college's new building, to be constructed on a vacant lot at 19 South Twenty-second Street. The boarding stable next to this lot was later torn down, creating space for the college's garden of medicinal plants. A building for the use of the Philadelphia congregation of the Swedenborgian General Church of the New Jerusalem (right), constructed in 1881 to a design by prominent Philadelphia architect Theophilus Parsons Chandler (1845–1928), still stands today as the college's nearest neighboring structure. Other important buildings by Cope and Stewardson grace the campuses of Princeton University, the University of Pennsylvania, Bryn Mawr College, and Washington University in St. Louis.

The laying of the cornerstone on the Twenty-second Street lot in 1908 commenced the construction of the college's second dedicated building. The huge quantities of gray granite blocks, red bricks, white limestone trim, and ornamental cast-iron girders delivered to the site over the following year would eventually result in one of Cope and Stewardson's most ornate "Jacobethan" constructions.

An important guest at the 1909 dedication ceremony for the completed Twenty-second Street building was steel magnate, entrepreneur, and philanthropist Andrew Carnegie (third from right), who donated most of the necessary funds for the college's second home. Carnegie's interest in the project resulted from his friendship with Mitchell (second from right).

The Twenty-second Street's building's rectangular shape is ornamented by projections and recesses, by color contrasts between the white limestone corners and the red brick, and by the distinctive and varied windows. The front and sides of the building are heavily decorated with columns, brackets, cartouches, and other rich ornamentation. The monumental wrought-iron front gate and fence surrounding the building are supported by brick and limestone piers. The limestone entrance posts flanking the gate are classical compositions of base, shaft, and capital. Over the front door are carved the name of The College of Physicians, the founding date of 1787, and the date of the building's completion, 1909. A century after its construction, the building became a National Historical Landmark, with the National Park Service describing it as "an outstanding property in the medical and cultural history of the United States."

The grand exterior doors open into a white marble vestibule whose walls are engraved with the names of many of the physicians who have been fellows of The College of Physicians of Philadelphia. The vestibule leads into an octagonal rotunda 30 feet in diameter. The rotunda serves as a temporary display area for changing exhibitions. One recent display celebrated the 200th anniversary of the Lewis and Clark Expedition. Titled "Only One Man Died: Medical Adventures on the Lewis and Clark Trail," this exhibit was unique among the hundreds of displays created for this national event, being the only one to focus on the health and medical aspects of this important story.

The rotunda leads to a grand staircase with a bronze railing. The first landing is dominated by a seven-foot-tall statue of Aesculapius, the Greek and Roman god of healing. This statue, a copy of a work in the Vatican that dates from the second century, was created by Philadelphia sculptor Carlo Manetti in 1911. Resting against the figure is the standard attribute of this god: the asklepian (rod of Aesculapius), a staff with a single serpent coiled around it. The snake symbolizes regeneration in classical European art—probably because of its apparent ability to rejuvenate by shedding old skin—so it is an appropriate emblem of healing. The modern use of the caduceus of Hermes (a winged rod with two snakes entwined around it) to symbolize the medical profession resulted from an erroneous substitution of the caduceus for the asklepian by the US Army Medical Corps in 1902. The error has persisted ever since.

During the 19th century, thousands of immigrants brought European classicism to the already well-established Philadelphia cabinetmaking industry. The marriage of European design and American craftsmanship produced much magnificent furniture in what is now known as the American Empire style. The Mütter Museum's beautiful display cases, most of which have been in use for over 100 years, were born of that marriage. In commissioning display cabinets to fit both the grand new building on Twenty-second Street as well as the unusual specimens of the museum, the college was able to put far more specimens on display than at the previous Locust Street location. Even after the advent of photography, anatomical specimens were—and still are—hugely important in the teaching of medicine.

Inspired by 17th-century English classicism, the Ashhurst Room is a grand space under a coved vaulted ceiling. Adjacent to the library, it formerly served as the library's reading room and still contains books on oak shelves and banks of oak card catalogue cabinets. These share wall space with oak wainscoting, recessed plaster panels, and doors crowned with pedimented gables. Today, this room is used primarily for lectures, meetings, and social gatherings. The clock at the top of the fireplace pediment, one of the first electric clocks in Philadelphia, is original to the building. This clock consists of a brass face set into a decorative plaster frieze. It has been running continuously (though not always accurately) since its installation in 1909.

The magnificent fireplace in the Ashhurst Room is flanked by a pair of Corinthian capitals enclosing a portrait of the man for whom this room is named: John Ashhurst Jr. (1839–1900), MD, FCPP. After working as an assistant surgeon during the Civil War, Ashhurst became an expert in orthopedic, vascular, and plastic surgery. He served as president of The College of Physicians of Philadelphia from 1898 to 1900 and bequeathed his large collection of medical books to the college's library. The college owns two oil portraits of Ashhurst, one by John Lambert Jr. (1861–1907) and the one that hangs over the fireplace in the Ashhurst Room, painted by Adolphe Borie (1877–1934). Both artists studied at the Pennsylvania Academy of the Fine Arts, the first art school in the United States, and both exhibited their work widely, participating in the national expositions at St. Louis in 1904 and San Francisco in 1915.

The upstairs vestibule has marble wainscoting, a cove cornice, and deeply paneled walls framing a few of the college's many important oil portraits. This space and the adjoining staircase are favorite photography venues for the many wedding parties celebrated in this building. The ornate leaded glass skylight in this photograph is now gone, but it might still be somewhere in the building. In 2011, electricians opened a long-closed utility room and discovered part of a leaded glass window stored inside. This newly discovered glass is not part of the lost skylight from the upstairs vestibule, but it offers hope that the lost skylight might yet be found.

The library's reading room in the new Twenty-second Street building is far more spacious than the reading room in the old Locust Street location. Each year, hundreds of scholars travel to Philadelphia from around the world to research the rich historical collections of the college's library and museum. This room, called the Norris Room after William Fisher Norris, MD, FCPP, is where those scholars do their work. The carved stone fireplace mantel in the library's reading room is the one architectural element of the old Locust Street building that was moved to the Twenty-second Street structure. Created by architect Theophilus Parsons Chandler, the man who designed the grand church that still stands on Twenty-second Street next to the college, the heavily sculpted overmantel showcases Chandler's love of the late French Gothic style.

The ceremonial heart of the building, Mitchell Hall, is more than 71 feet long and 48 feet wide. This huge room boasts richly carved oak wainscoting, carved pilasters, pedimented doors, and a plaster cove cornice. Here is where the formal induction of new fellows occurs, with the governing officials overseeing the ceremony from their seats at the mahogany rostrum. The rostrum's carved details include the college's founding date of 1787 and the date of its first building, 1863. This grand room is a fitting tribute to the man who was largely responsible for the construction of this magnificent building: Silas Weir Mitchell, MD, FCPP.

Three

THE HISTORICAL
MEDICAL LIBRARY

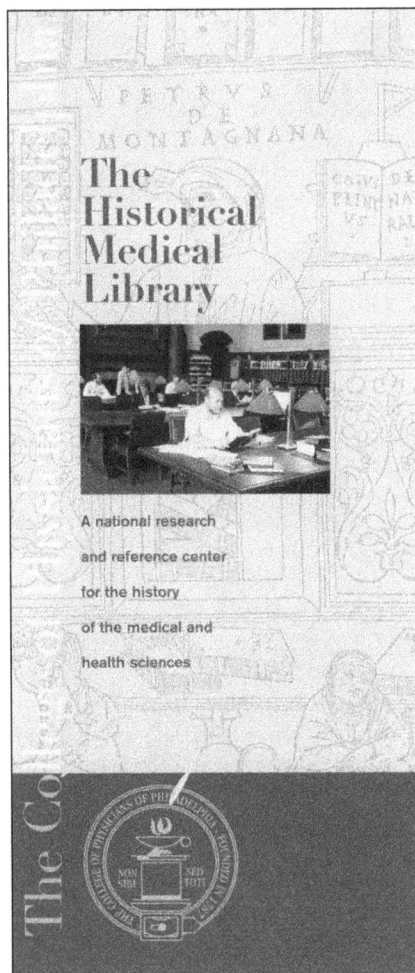

The Historical Medical Library of The College of Physicians of Philadelphia is one of the world's premier research collections on the history of medicine. The rare holdings of the library include an extensive collection of manuscripts and archives and a comprehensive collection of 19th- and early-20th-century medical journals. The library actively highlights its collections in lectures, fellowships, public programs, and publications.

Of particular significance within the archives of The College of Physicians of Philadelphia are opinions given by fellows of the college during the yellow fever epidemic of 1793, the documents establishing the Mütter Museum, the campaign to construct the Twenty-second Street building, and the vast correspondence to Charles Perry Fisher, library superintendent from 1882 to 1932.

Thomas Grier Miller (1886–1981), MD, FCPP, president of The College of Physicians of Philadelphia during 1949–1951, was a driving force behind the development of the library. He built financial support and formed a committee that undertook physical repairs to the building. He also created a network of lawyers, bankers, and civic leaders to advise the college on fundraising and to introduce the library to the general public.

The Francis Clark Wood Institute for the History of Medicine was established in 1976 to promote the rich historical resources of the college's library and museum. During the academic year, the institute sponsors seminars and major conferences, such as "A Melancholy Scene of Devastation: The Public Response to the 1793 Philadelphia Yellow Fever Epidemic." It also provides travel grants to researchers who require the use of the college's collections of texts, manuscripts, archives, images, artifacts, and specimens in the history of medicine. Dozens of worthy projects have resulted from research sponsored by the Wood Institute, including a museum exhibit on the role of women in medicine, an academic paper on the esthetics of medical museums, a scholarly monograph on physiognomy, a biography of Silas Weir Mitchell, and a film on the relationship between body modification and the perception of beauty. Recent grantees have traveled to Philadelphia from England, Canada, Missouri, Louisiana, Massachusetts, North Carolina, and Illinois.

Among the first items acquired by the library was the founding book of modern pathology, *De sedibus et causis morborum* ("On the Seats and Causes of Disease"), written by Giambattista Morgagni and published in Venice in 1761. Morgagni presented an inscribed copy to John Morgan, MD, FCPP, during a visit to Padua, Italy. Morgan, a founding member of the college and the person most responsible for the establishment of the nation's first medical school at the University of Pennsylvania, later donated this valuable book to the college. *De sedibus* is now a medical classic, and the college's copy is the seed from which its magnificent rare book collection has grown.

The Historical Medical Digital Library features electronic selections from books significant in the history of medicine. Patrons may browse the digital library in order to see frontispieces, title pages, dedications, selected portions of texts, illustrations, and tables of contents. The digital library was developed with a grant from the Institute of Museum and Library Services. Copyright for the digital resources of The College of Physicians of Philadelphia is in the public domain. These resources are intended for the personal use of patrons and as a resource for educational institutions. Some of the most important titles include the 1643 London edition of Sir Thomas Browne's *Religio medici*, the 1745 Philadelphia edition of Thomas Cadwalader's *An Essay on the West-India Dry-Gripes* (printed by Benjamin Franklin), and the 1573 Paris edition of Ambroise Paré's *Deux Livres de Chirurgie*. (AB early medical handbooks.)

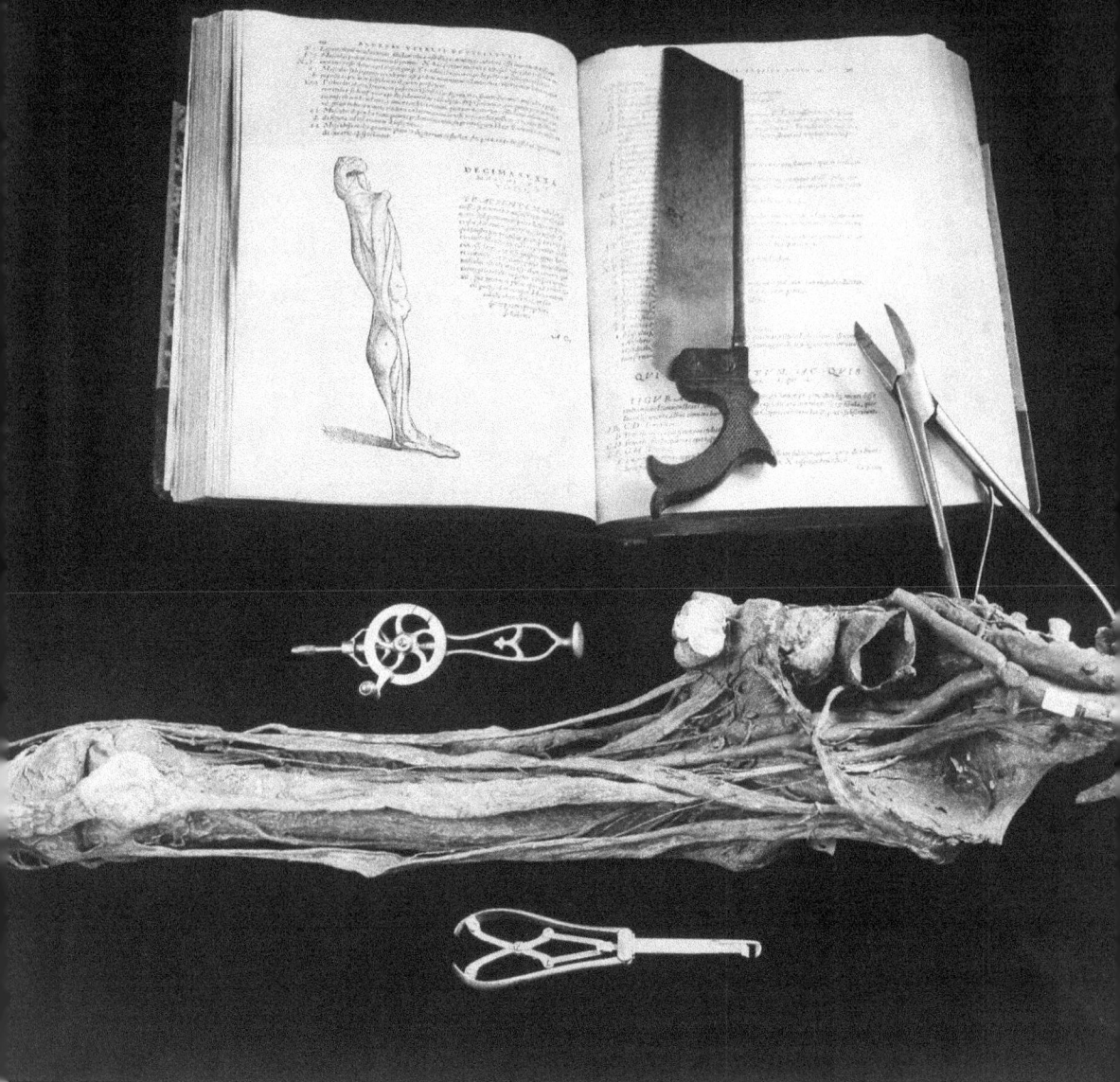

The library also offers two fully searchable, digitized editions of 18th-century Pennsylvania medical manuscripts. The *Medicina Pennsylvania* was written by George de Benneville, a Huguenot practitioner who probably trained in Germany. The *Remediorum specimina* was written by Abraham Wagner, a member of the Schwenkfelders, a religious sect that arose in Silesia in the early years of the Protestant reformation. The de Benneville manuscript is owned by The College of Physicians of Philadelphia; the Wagner has been made available by the Schwenkfelder Library of Pennsburg, Pennsylvania. This digitization project was made possible by a grant from the National Library of Medicine to Prof. Renate Wilson of the Bloomberg School of Public Health of the Johns Hopkins University. (AB.)

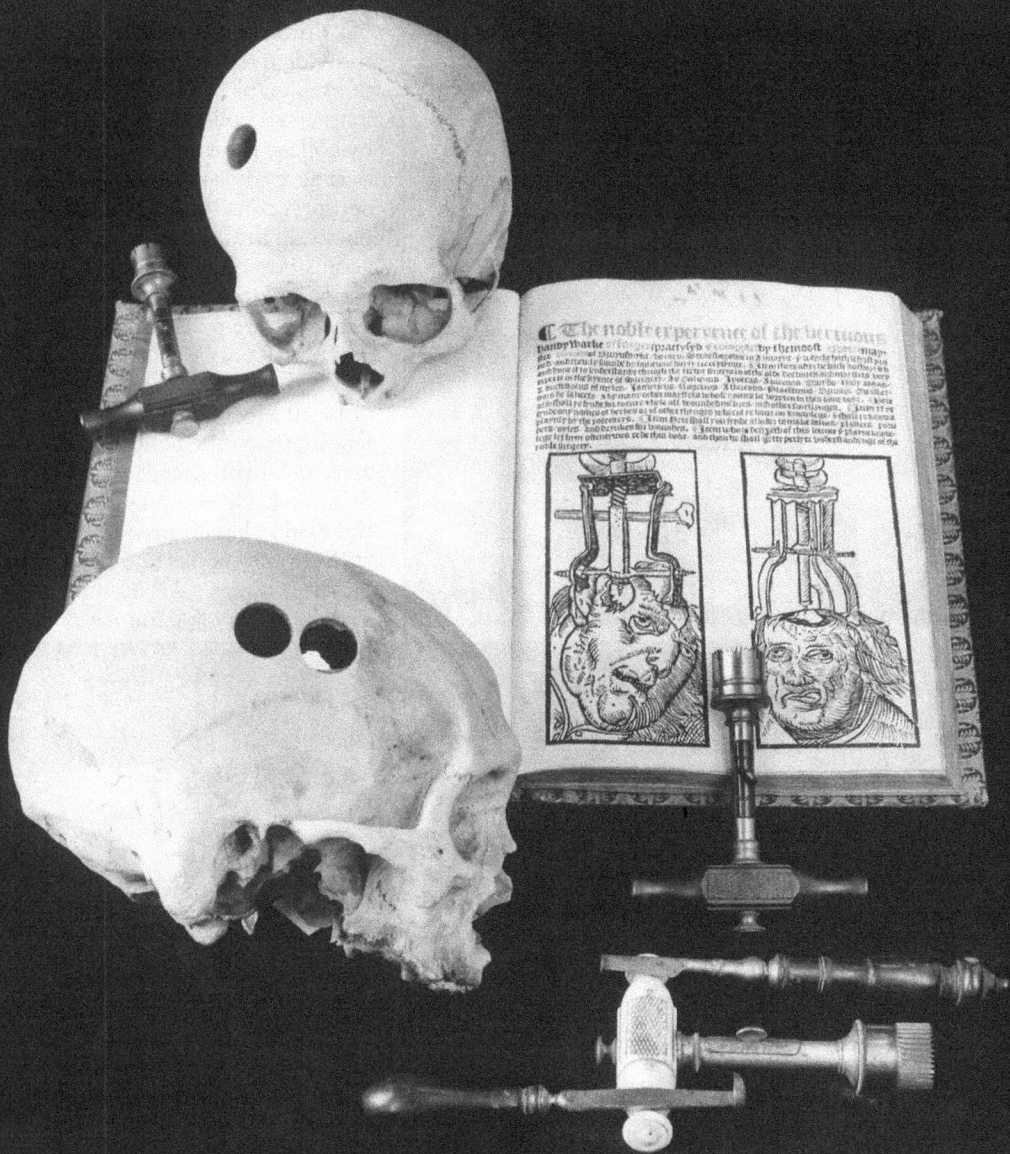

In addition to its rare books and 19th- and 20th-century collections, the college's library is notable for its manuscripts and archives. Within this collection are the college's own archives and those of other Philadelphia medical institutions as well as letters, case books, and student notebooks that document the personal lives and professional practice of doctors in the Philadelphia region and around the world. Among the most important manuscript collections are the bulk of the extant letters written by Silas Weir Mitchell, MD, FCPP, Civil War surgeon, neurologist, physiologist, novelist, and leading member of the college for more than 50 years. (AB texts and apparatus relating to trephination.)

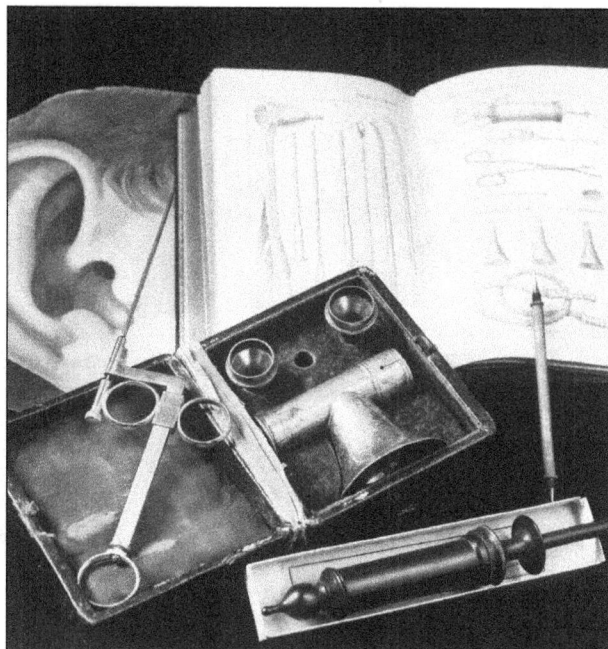

The library owns several collections of printed books associated with individual fellows of The College of Physicians of Philadelphia. The Lewis collections, donated by college president Samuel Lewis over several decades in the 19th century, consist of several thousand books, many of them rare, whose acquisition clearly established the singular importance of the library. More recently, forensic psychiatrist Robert L. Sadoff, MD, FCPP, donated the Sadoff Library of Legal Medicine and Forensic Psychiatry to the college. Before arriving at the college in 2002, Sadoff's 4,000 volumes comprised the world's largest private collection of books and pamphlets on these topics. (AB otoscopes and optometry apparatus.)

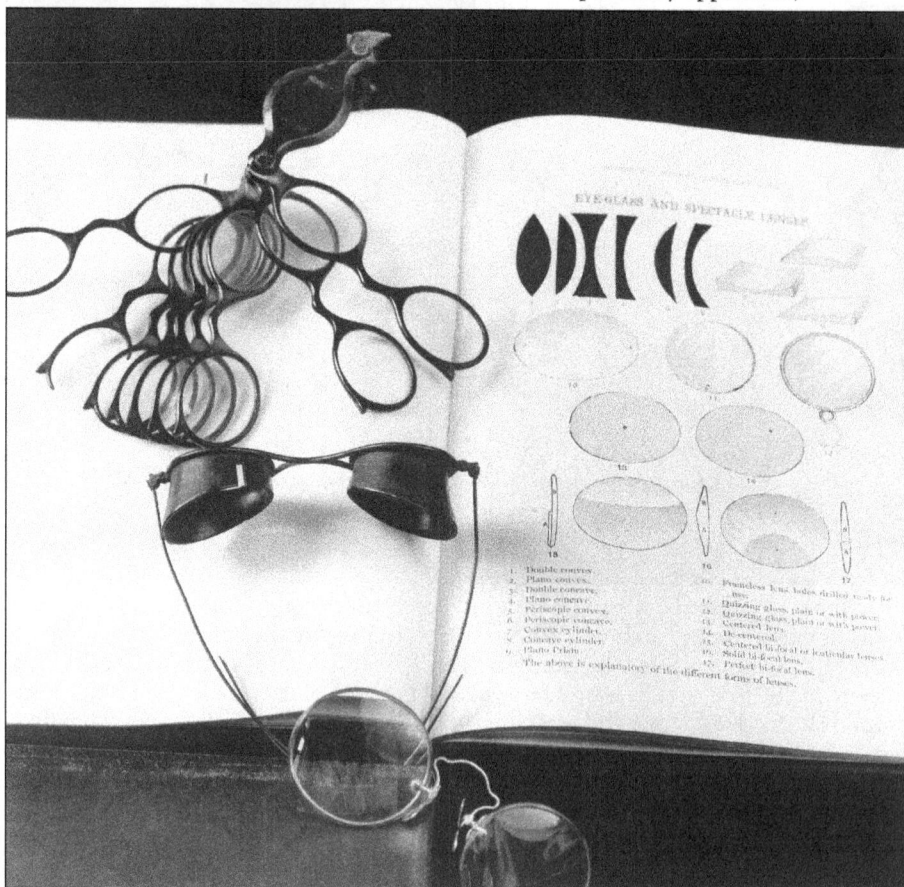

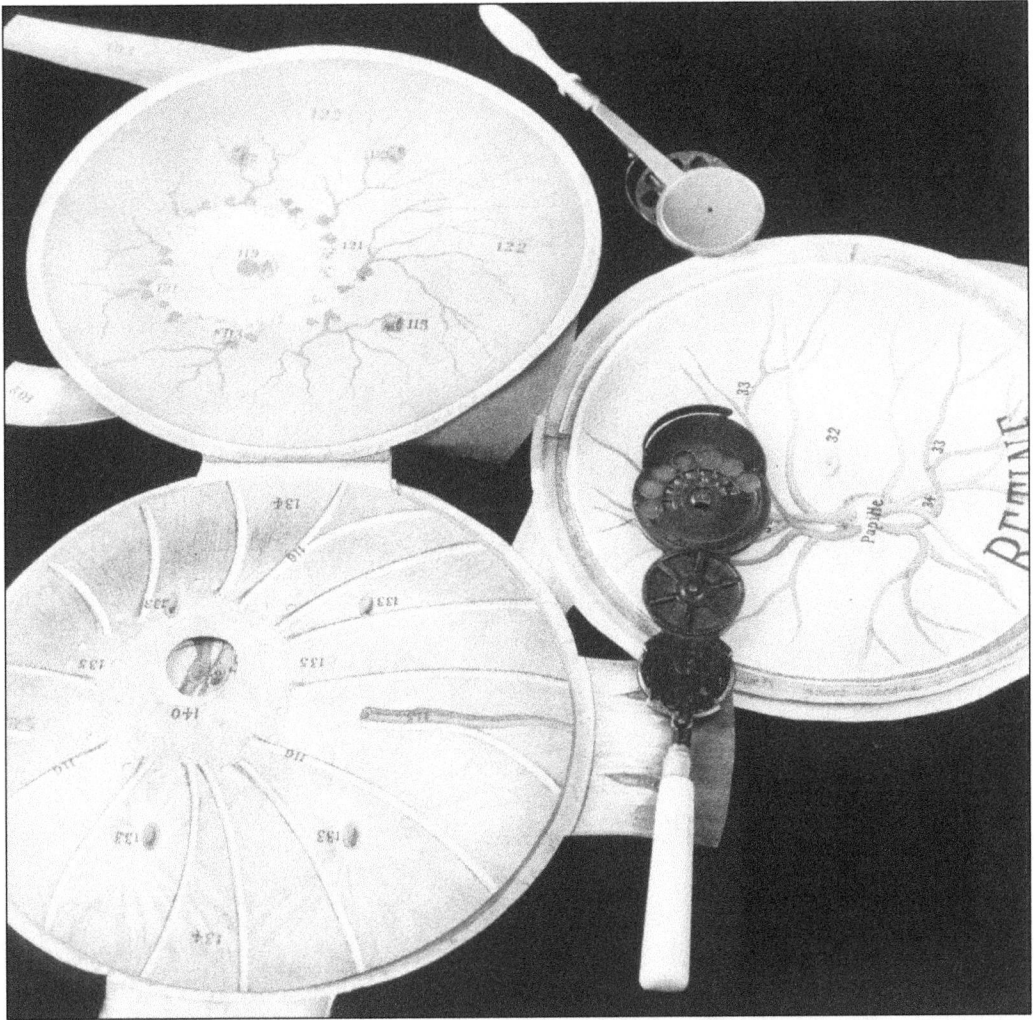

The library functioned as Philadelphia's central medical library from the 1850s to the 1970s, serving its medical schools, hospitals, physicians, and other health professionals. During much of the 20th century, the library also served as the Mid-Atlantic Regional Medical Library of the National Network of Libraries of Medicine. It was redesignated a historical library in 1996, formalizing its specialized function as a repository for the history of medicine. The historical materials interest students of history, sociology, anthropology, literature, visual art, and political science—subjects that now overlap medicine in the modern specialty of medical humanities. Furthermore, a few experiments to expose high school students and undergraduates to the library show promise. Today's high school students have grown up with no experience of large institutional library collections, so the college's collection is a novelty. Books such as early anatomical atlases are stimulating younger researchers. The future of the library now lies in creating, sustaining, and expanding an electronic presence. (AB apparatus for retinal examination.)

The library's holdings include more than 400 books printed before 1500. Of these, 33 are the only copies of their titles in North America. Thanks to a recent grant from the William Penn Foundation, the college can claim the best-cataloged collection of early books in the world. Among more than 12,000 other rare books are most of those that laid the groundwork of modern medicine, including one of the world's best copies of William Harvey's 1628 *De motu cordis* ("On the Motion of the Heart"), the first book to describe the circulation of the blood. The library also holds two copies of the 1543 *De humani corporis fabrica* ("On the Material of the Human Body") by Andreas Vesalius, the book that was the foundation of both modern anatomy and modern medical illustration. Pictured here is the 1778 edition of *Tabulae sceleti et musculorum corporis humani* by Bernhard Siegfried Albinus. (AB.)

The Historical Medical Library of The College of Physicians of Philadelphia has established partnerships with kindred institutions in order to create the world's largest and most accessible collection of digital resources in the history of medicine: The Medical Heritage Library. These partner institutions include the university libraries of Harvard, Yale, Columbia, and Johns Hopkins as well as the National Library of Medicine, the New York Academy of Medicine, and London's Wellcome Trust. Pictured here are early X-ray texts and apparatus along with a physician's bookplate presenting an X-ray view of the human body. (Right, AB.)

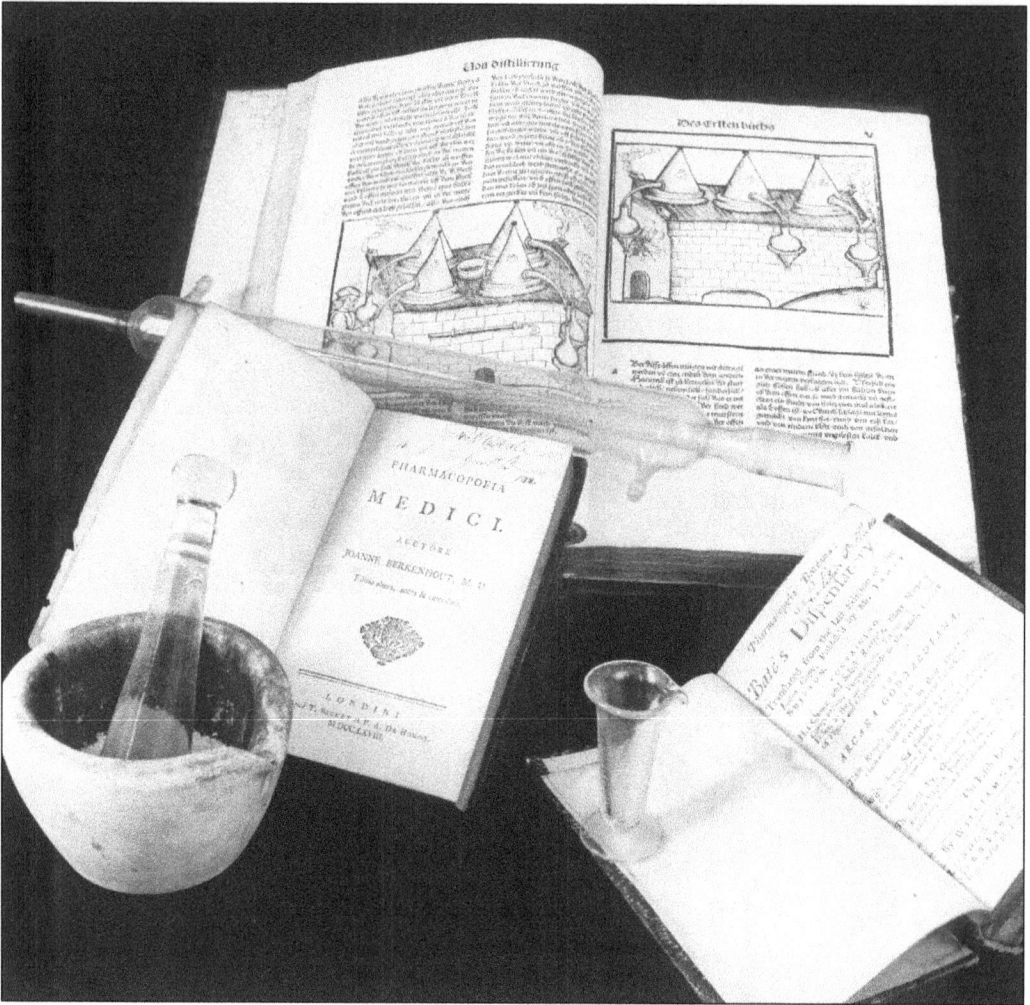

Care of the library collections has always been of great concern to The College of Physicians of Philadelphia. Monitoring and controlling environmental conditions are essential for reducing the deterioration of all books and papers, particularly old ones. Fluctuating temperatures and humidity levels, light, dirt, microorganisms, insects, old tape and glue used for repairs—all these can lessen the lifespan of any paper object. The college recently installed a state-of-the-art climate control system in the library stacks, and several recent grants and gifts have been applied to an extensive preservation and restoration program. (AB books on distillation.)

The Historical Medical Library of The College of Physicians of Philadelphia shows its lighter side in collections of paper ephemera: advertisements, brochures, trade catalogues, and other printed material intended for brief use. This postcard is the work of British illustrator Donald McGill, active during World War I. At the peak of McGill's popularity, over 16 million copies of his postcards were sold each year.

"BADLY HIT ——— CONDITION SERIOUS !"

Sérieusement atteint—état grave!

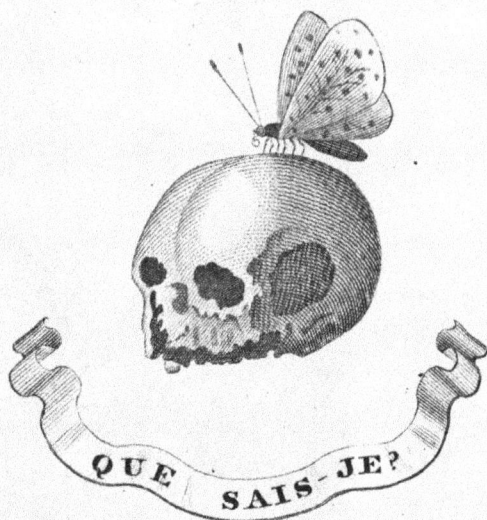

QUE SAIS-JE?

Sam.l Lewis M.D.

The books in the collection of Samuel Lewis, MD, FCPP, are marked with Lewis's bookplate: an image of a skull (symbol of mortality) crowned by a butterfly (symbol of the soul), both underlined by a banner reading "Que sais-je?" ("What do I know"?), a tribute to the great Renaissance essayist Michel de Montaigne. This combination of symbolic pictorial image and motto is an emblem, a personal form of art more than 400 years old.

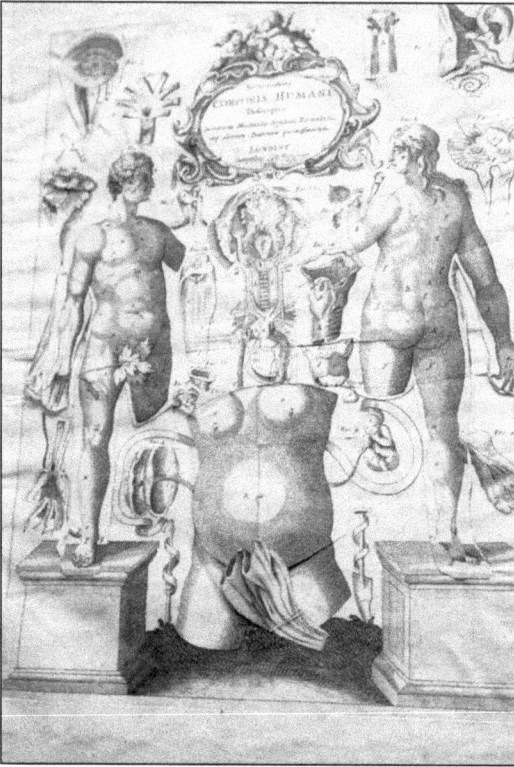

Cataptrum microcosmicum ("A Survey of the Microcosm: Or, The Anatomy of the Bodies of Man and Woman"), first published in 1619 by John Remmelin, contains highly detailed anatomical illustrations of female and male human bodies. The reader can open many layers of flaps on each image, performing a virtual dissection. Remmelin conceived the idea of a layered anatomy text while serving as a physician in Ulm, Germany. He wanted to create a book that could show the relationship of muscles, bones, and internal organs to each other. The illustrations were created by printing many separate images, cutting them out, and pasting them together in three-dimensional order. This process resulted in as many as 15 successive layers in a single image, each revealing a new, deeper level of the human anatomy.

Four

MEDICAL ADVANCES

In the dissecting room at the University of Pennsylvania School of Medicine (c. 1900), medical students pose with their subjects of study. The legality of human dissection for medical education has varied throughout history, and surgeons have often had to rely on a supply of executed criminals to meet their demand. The pressure from rapidly growing medical schools in the mid-18th century led to a black market in cadavers and body parts for dissection.

The Medical Department of Jefferson Hospital was established in Philadelphia in 1825 (against the efforts of the University of Pennsylvania to maintain its status as the only medical college in town), eventually becoming Jefferson Medical College in 1838. Silas Weir Mitchell, MD, FCPP, graduated from Jefferson in 1850. In 1877, Jefferson opened one of the first hospitals in America associated with a medical school and strove to improve the standard of hospital facilities.

The care of hospital patients in the 18th and 19th centuries usually involved fresh air and plenty of time outdoors. The gardens of hospitals built during this period were constructed to be destinations for patients, not merely scenery. Modern research shows that exposure to daylight does reduce the risk of depression during recovery and being outside in a garden lowers patient stress.

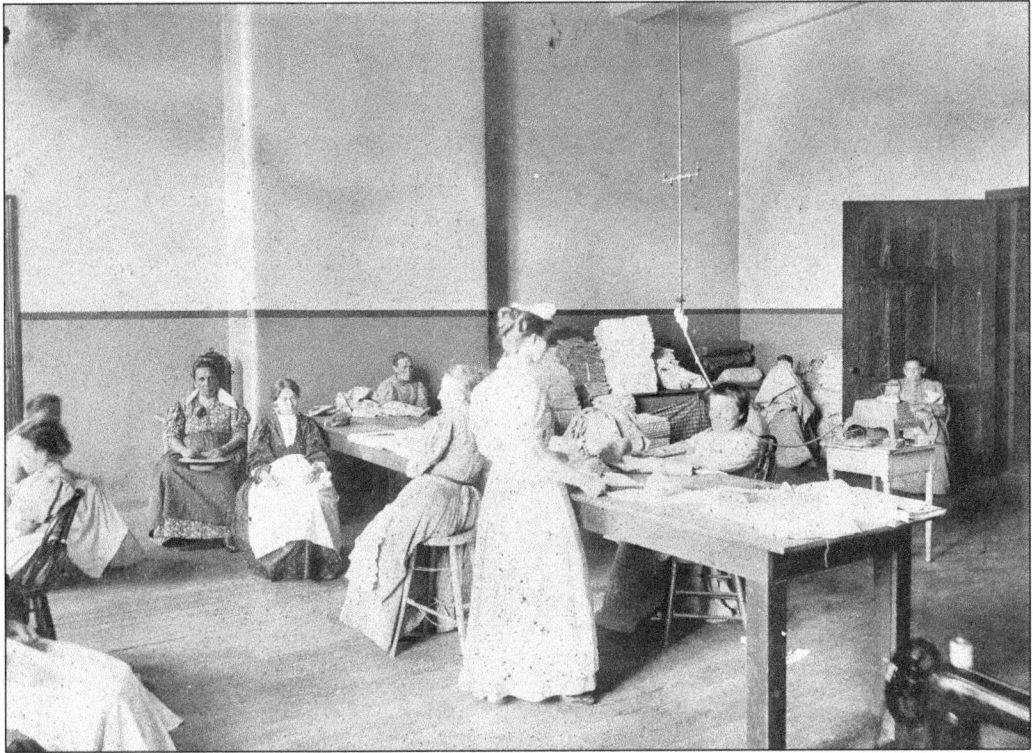

Many 19th-century hospitals depended on the labor of their patients to function. Those who were able-bodied worked on farms; served in workshops, kitchens, and laundries; and cleaned the wards. Each hospital baked its own bread, washed its own laundry, and made and repaired the clothes and shoes of the patients. Hospital workshops manufactured goods such as brushes and tinware. Patients were at first paid with tokens or cigarettes and later with money.

The brass band of Old Blockley provided an early version of music therapy. For at least 1,000 years, music has been documented as useful in treating mood disorders. Current scholarly research demonstrates that music therapy can also improve cognitive functioning, motor skills, emotional development, and social skills. As a universal human behavior, the making and enjoyment of music functions as a unifying and reassuring activity.

The Blockley Band
circa 1867
Roberts, Luhring, Beecher, standing;
Means, Curtin, Stryker, below;

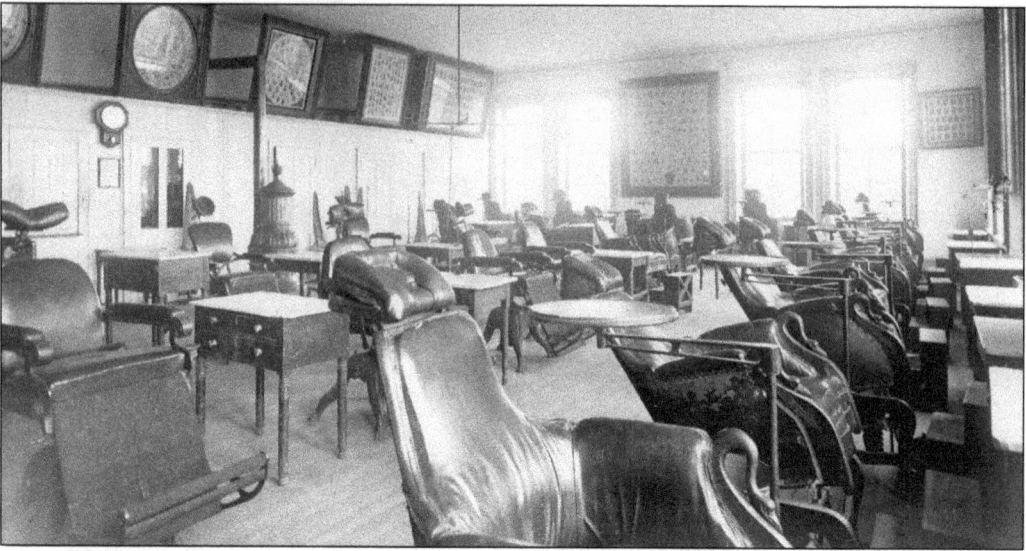

For several centuries, minor surgical procedures such as bloodletting and tooth extractions were performed by barbers, with the traditional pole striped in red and white (symbolizing the blood and bandages involved in these procedures) serving to advertise the location of the barber's shop. Even as late as the end of the 19th century, minor surgeries were still being performed on patients seated in barber's chairs rather than lying on a table. When the observation of surgical procedures became an important part of a medical student's education, surgical theaters evolved. The positioning of the patient on a table rather than in a chair helped the spectators observe the operation as clearly as possible. The operating surgeon in this surgical theater is Jacob da Silva Solis-Cohen, MD, FCPP.

Before refrigeration, hospitals relied on food that could be transported and stored in cans and barrels. Since many patients were malnourished or undernourished, physicians frequently prescribed large meals, sometimes six a day. Patients ate meat and potatoes, heavily buttered bread, and sugared pastries. They were also prescribed sugared beverages (such as tea and cocoa) and alcoholic beverages (such as port wine, sherry, stout, and ale).

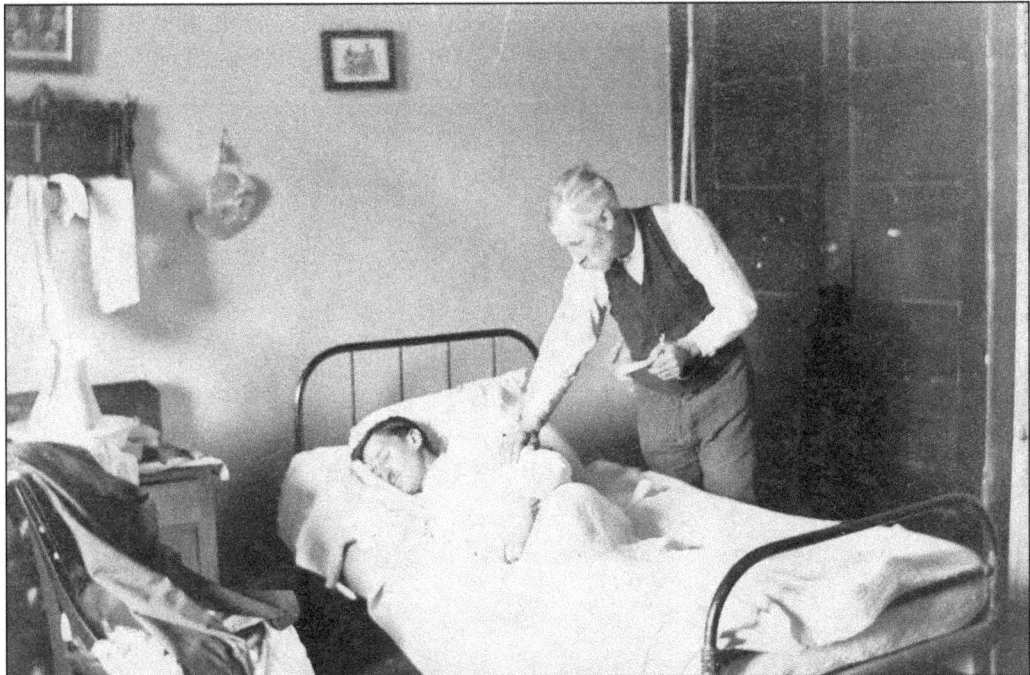

Until telephones were common, resident physicians on night duty in hospitals were notified by messenger when medical advice was required by interns or nurses. If his presence was not required for a medical emergency, the physician sent his response by the same messenger.

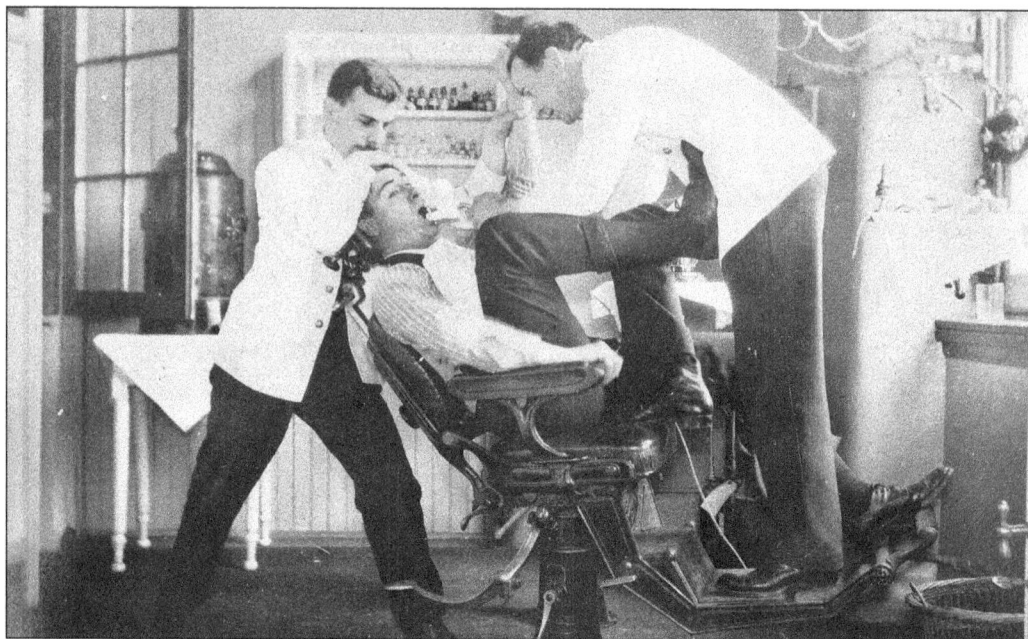

Before modern anesthesia, surgery was a risky last resort for illness and injury. The pain and invasiveness of surgical procedures often caused patients to go into shock, and the risk of infection or death was high. Plant-based anesthetics were sometimes used, but their results were unpredictable. Alcohol and opium were the most popular anesthetics, but the amount of alcohol required to render a patient insensible had negative consequences, and opium was not a strong enough painkiller to suffice for most surgeries. Morphine became an option for anesthesia in the mid-19th century, followed by nitrous oxide, diethyl ether, and chloroform. These two staged photographs show a patient undergoing a dental procedure with and without anesthesia.

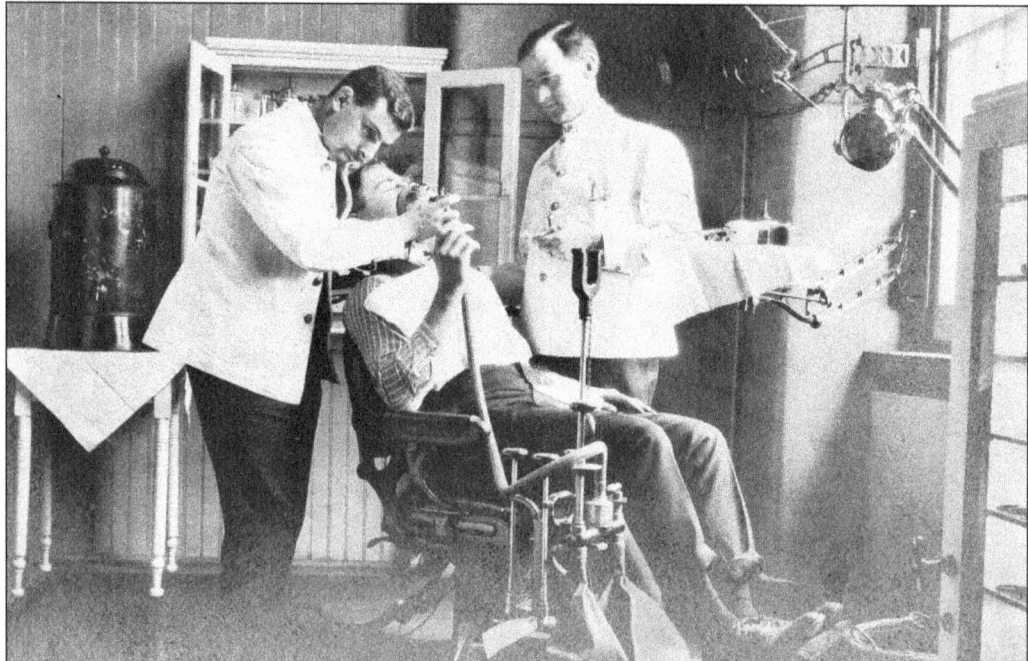

This staged photograph of an operating theater dates from c. 1888, when the use of diethyl ether as an anesthetic was very popular. The anesthetist covers the patient's mouth and nose with an ether cone while the surgeon prepares to amputate the lower right leg. Ether was first used as a medical anesthetic in 1842 by Crawford Long, MD, who published his findings in 1849. The first known surgical use of ether in Philadelphia occurred in 1846, when Thomas Dent Mütter, MD, FCPP, performed surgery on an etherized patient for the removal of a tumor from a cheek. Shortly thereafter, Philadelphia's first obstetrical delivery under ether was directed by John K. Mitchell, MD, FCPP (the father of Silas Weir Mitchell, MD, FCPP).

Heinrich Hermann Robert Koch, MD (1843–1910), one of the founders of microbiology, was awarded the Nobel Prize for isolating the tuberculosis bacillus in 1882. He also isolated the bacteria responsible for anthrax and cholera. Using Koch's methods, his students found the organisms responsible for diphtheria, typhoid, pneumonia, gonorrhea, cerebrospinal meningitis, Hansen's disease (leprosy), bubonic plague, tetanus, and syphilis.

Predating the American Revolution by over four decades, the Blockley Almshouse was one of the first public hospitals on the North American continent. "Old Blockley" was renamed Philadelphia General Hospital in 1919, and this photograph shows its biochemistry laboratory the following year. When this hospital closed in 1977, it left many of its archives to The College of Physicians of Philadelphia.

Two decades after the introduction of anesthetics to surgery, Sir Joseph Lister introduced sterile technique (antisepsis). In 1865, he showed that sterilizing metal instruments by heat could greatly reduce infection after medical procedures. He also promoted frequent hand-washing and clean linens to reduce risks even more. At about the same time, Koch introduced a procedure to clean medical instruments by steam to eliminate bacteria. Soon, all surfaces and instruments were routinely sterilized before and during surgical operations. (AB texts on consumption and irrigating syringes.)

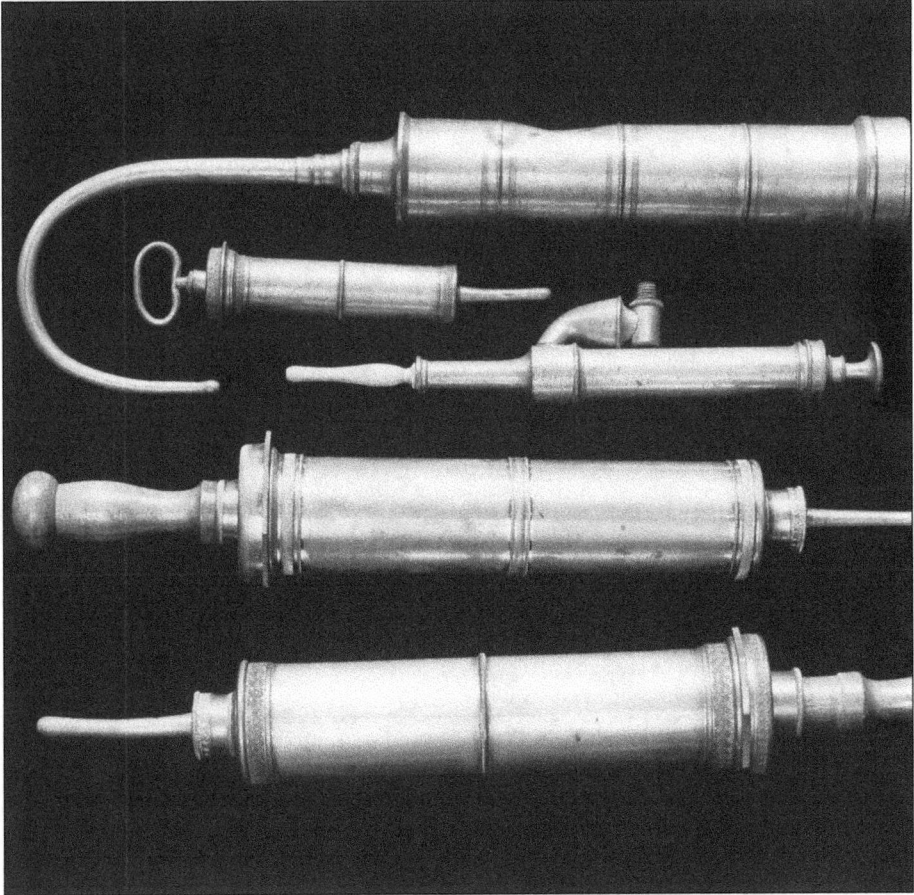

One of the oldest African American universities in the United States is Shaw University, founded in Raleigh, North Carolina, in 1865. Shaw's medical school was founded in 1881, the first four-year medical school in the South to train black physicians and pharmacists. Although this photograph of one of Shaw's earliest medical classes shows only male graduates, by 1900 Shaw was educating male and female medical students in roughly equal numbers.

Although women attended clinical lectures and participated in anatomy classes as early as 1850, they were initially viewed as less competent physicians than men. The long struggle to place female physicians in hospitals was aided by several eminent physicians who were fellows of The College of Physicians of Philadelphia, including Joseph Leidy, Silas Weir Mitchell, and William W. Keen. Mary Pauline Root, shown here as an intern, was the first woman in Pennsylvania to receive an appointment as a resident physician.

Founded in 1850, the Female (later Woman's) Medical College of Pennsylvania was the world's first medical college for women. Ann Preston, MD, became dean in 1866, the first woman ever to hold that position at any medical school. The college began accepting male students in 1970, merged with Hahnemann University in 1993, and is now the Drexel College of Medicine. This is the 1914–1915 class of the Woman's Medical College of Pennsylvania.

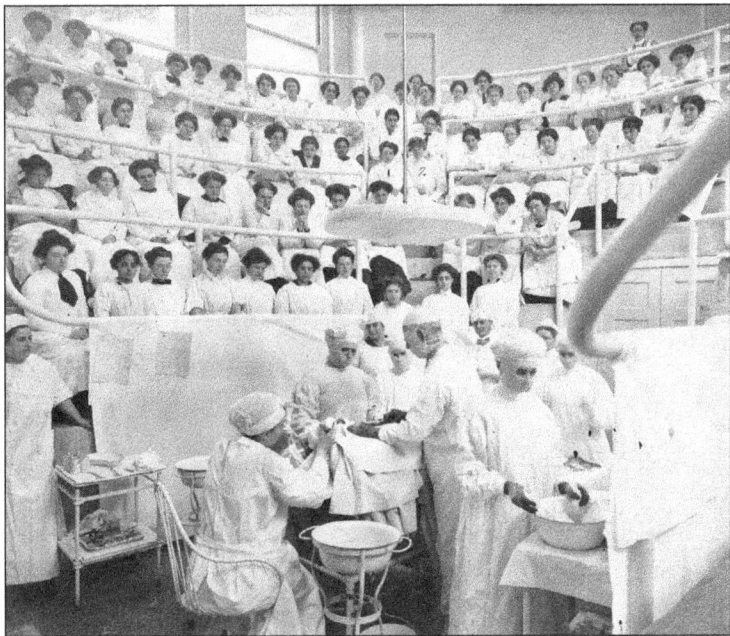

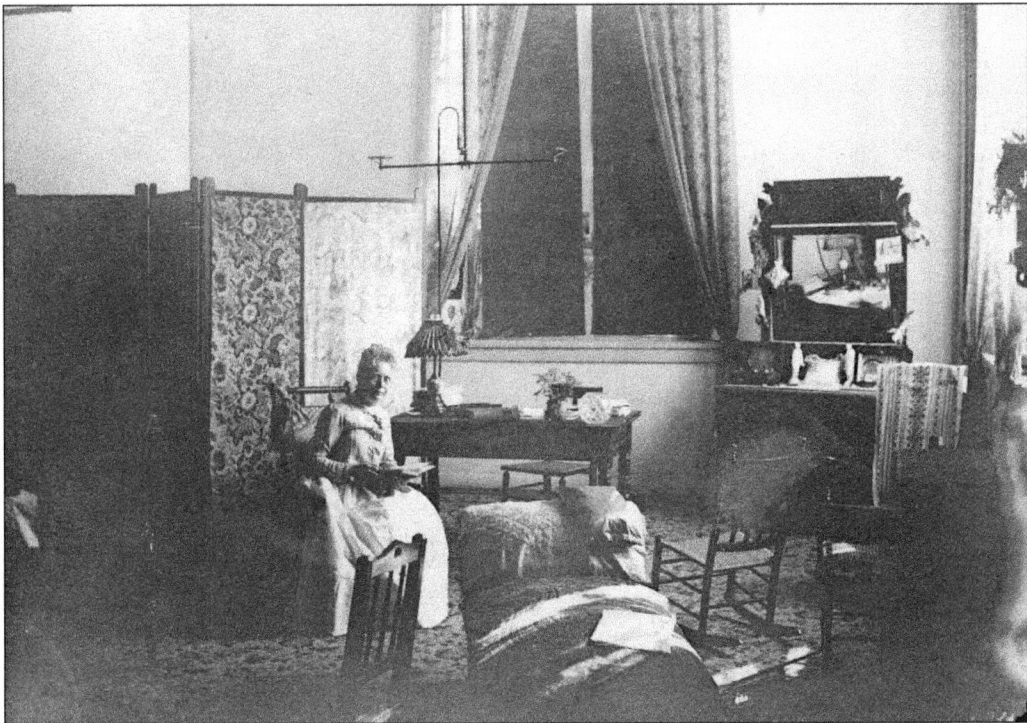

Amelia Gilman, MD (shown here c. 1888), served as resident physician at Old Blockley, eventually becoming head of the Female Insane Ward. The 19th-century medical definitions of "insanity" were much broader than they are today, including conditions such as alcoholism, epilepsy, and depression—chronic conditions that were not easily treated before the advent of new therapies in the mid-20th century. Gilman also appears in the photograph of Osler's autopsy class.

Wilhelm Conrad Röntgen (1845–1923) revolutionized medicine with his discovery of the medical use of X-rays. Although other researchers preceded him in working with X-rays, it was Röntgen who determined the travel pattern, travel distance, and penetrating capability of the rays. When the first known medical X-ray photograph (taken by Röntgen of his wife's hand) was publicly released in 1896, medical practitioners around the world immediately understood the enormous potential of this technology: For the first time ever, physicians could now look into a patient's body without cutting into it. This bronze bust of Röntgen was created by Christabel Cummings (born mid-19th century).

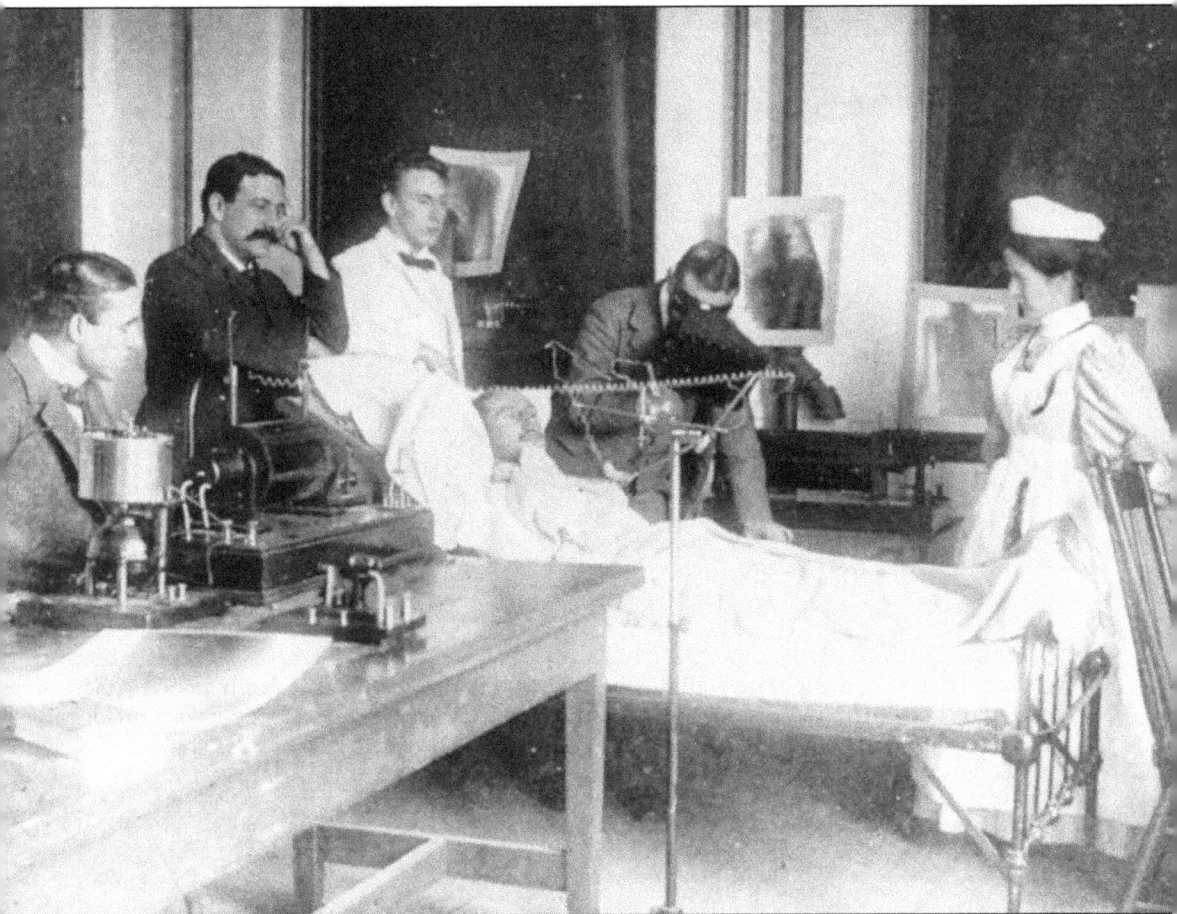

The benefits of X-ray technology to modern medical practice have been enormous. Now, countless internal medical imaging studies are performed worldwide each year. X-ray technology has enabled medical practitioners to detect pneumonia, heart failure, intestinal blockage, tooth decay, and other diseases. Millions of patients with cancer have been helped with radiation therapy. In addition, X-rays enabled biophysicist Rosalind Franklin to discover the double helical structure of DNA through diffraction imaging, thus laying the groundwork for modern genetic research.

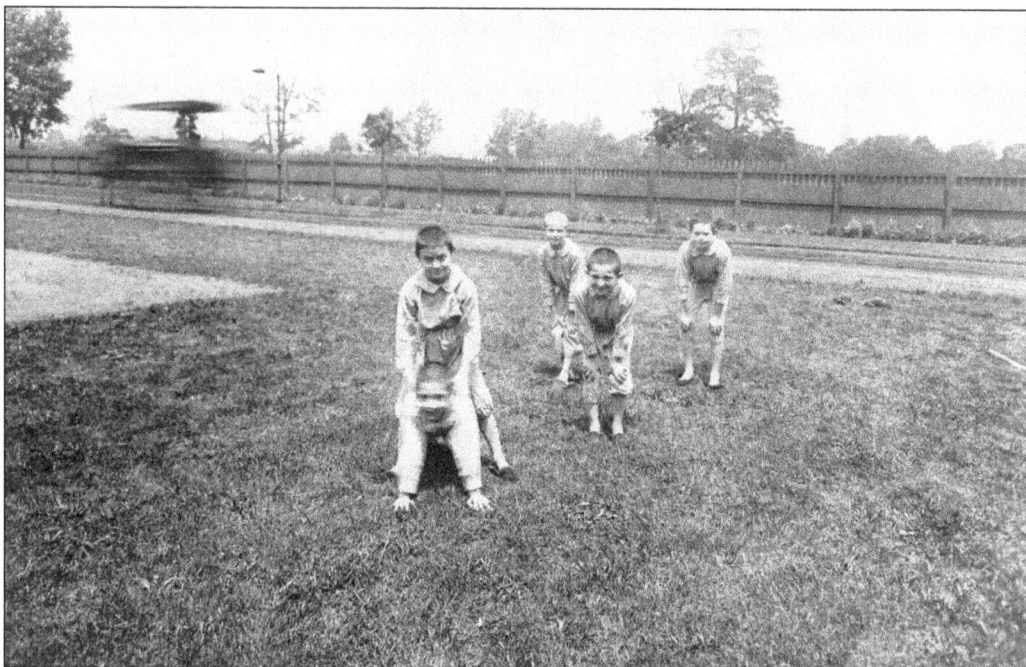

Before the development of penicillin, scarlet fever was a major cause of death among American children. This 1917 photograph shows children recovering from scarlet fever outside Philadelphia General Hospital. As part of their medical treatment, their heads have been shaved, allowing physicians to reduce the fever by applying ice to the scalp.

Artist Dean Cornwell shakes the hand of Col. C.M. Watson in front of Cornwell's 1943 painting *Conquerors of Yellow Fever.* The first years of work on the Panama Canal were disastrous because of the high rate of yellow fever among the laborers. The discovery that the disease is transmitted by mosquitoes laid the groundwork for modern epidemiology (the study of how, why, and where diseases occur).

Five

ACCOMPLISHMENTS
OF THE FELLOWS

This bill for medical services performed in 1786 by Benjamin Rush, MD, FCPP, lists a charge of £3 for vaccinating a child against smallpox. One of Rush's friends, Benjamin Franklin, became an eloquent proponent of vaccination after the death of his four-year-old son from smallpox: "I long regretted bitterly and still regret that I had not given [immunity] to him by inoculation."

The first medical school in North America was the Medical School of the College of Philadelphia, later to become the University of Pennsylvania. Its 1887 medical faculty consisted of (1) William Pepper, (2) Joseph Leidy, (3) Richard A.F. Penrose, (4) Alfred Stillé, (5) D. Hayes Agnew, (6) William Goodell, (7) James Tyson, (8) Horatio C. Wood, (9) Theodore G. Wormley, (10) John Ashhurst, and (11) Harrison Allen. All except Pepper and Penrose were fellows of The College of Physicians of Philadelphia.

The founder of professional medical illustration in the United States was Hermann Faber (1832–1913). Primarily known for being the only artist allowed to sit at Lincoln's deathbed to sketch the scene, Faber was a German immigrant who was granted citizenship for his service with the Army Medical Corps during the Civil War. He is shown here c. 1880.

Hermann Faber's son, Erwin Faber (1866–1939), became a medical illustrator like his father, preparing over 600 images to illustrate medical textbooks written by University of Pennsylvania faculty. In this c. 1908 image, with John Heisler preparing the specimen, Faber works on a postmortem illustration.

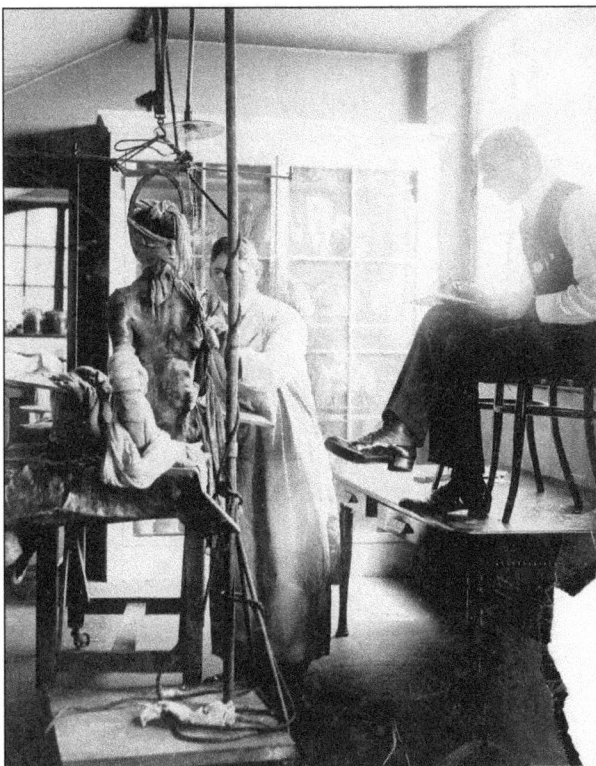

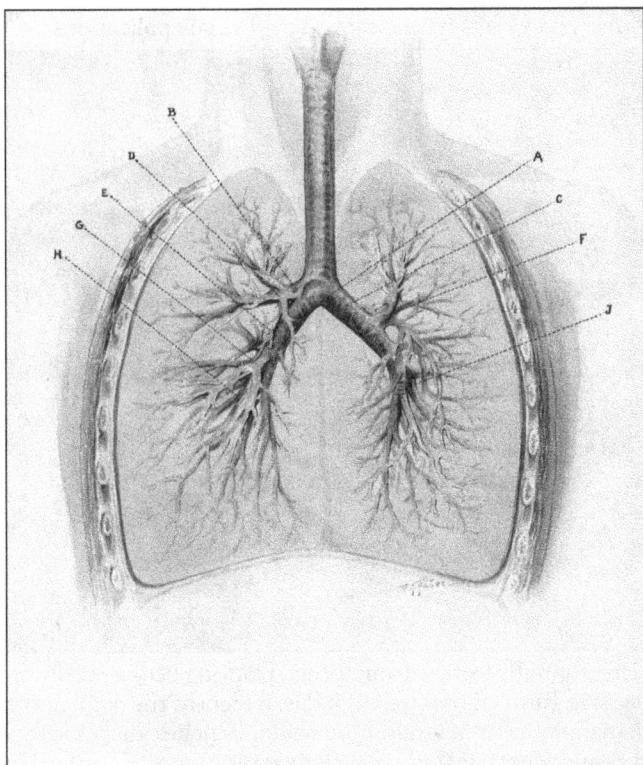

Even after the advent of photography, medical illustration was essential in teaching anatomy to students. Illustrations could be manipulated for clarity and edited for relevance in a way that photographs could not. Here is Erwin Faber's ink and watercolor illustration of the lung's bronchial tree (c. 1931), one of dozens of such illustrations owned by The College of Physicians of Philadelphia.

Benjamin Rush, MD, FCPP, envisioned the creation of a medicinal plant garden. In his era of practice, plant-derived medicines were important, though their curative powers remained mysterious. His vision was finally achieved in 1937, when the college celebrated its 150th anniversary by creating just such a garden. Visitors to the college are interested to discover that many familiar plants (such as dandelion, foxglove, mint, and violet) have long had medicinal applications.

Open free to the public daily, the garden originally featured four formal planting beds containing 50 medicinal plants used in the Americas in Rush's day as well as today. Recently, the garden was expanded to include even more medicinal plants from around the world. Benches allow visitors to sit in sun or shade to enjoy the sights and scents of this private city oasis.

George Bacon Wood (1797–1879), MD, FCPP, served as president of The College of Physicians of Philadelphia for three decades, from 1849 until his death. Along with Franklin Bache, he published the first edition (1833) of *The Dispensatory of the United States*, which soon became the national standard of uniformity for the prescription and dispensation of medicinal drugs. The college's library holds a copy of this first edition.

Another of Rush's accomplishments was the establishment of the Philadelphia Dispensary (1786–1922) for the medical relief of the poor, the first institution of its kind in the United States. Supported by private contributions, the dispensary offered free medical services and medications to those who could not afford to pay.

Sir William Osler (1849–1919), MD, FCPP, revolutionized the medical teaching system in the United States. Unlike his predecessors in medical education, Osler minimized lectures, instead requiring his students to learn through practical exercises, such as this autopsy. The photograph dates between 1884 and 1889, the years when Osler (seated in center) was chair of Clinical Medicine at the University of Pennsylvania. While living in Philadelphia, Osler enthusiastically assisted in expanding the library holdings of The College of Physicians of Philadelphia by donating many of the rare medical books for which the library is famous. The charcoal sketch of Osler was made by John Singer Sargent (1856–1925), widely acclaimed as the best American portraitist of his generation. The rough, unfinished background and clothing contrast dramatically with the beautifully finished head, creating a sense of tension and energy.

Philip Syng Physick (1768–1837), MD, FCPP, investigated the cause and treatment of the yellow fever epidemic of 1793 and was one of the first physicians to understand that this disease was not transmitted from person to person or through "bad air." One of his most important patients was the first chief justice of the United States, John Marshall (1755–1835). Marshall's opinions laid the basis for American constitutional law and made the Supreme Court of the United States a branch of government coequal with the legislative and executive branches. A few of the hundreds of bladder stones that Physick removed from Marshall in 1831 are maintained as a specimen by the Mütter Museum. This portrait of Physick was painted by Robert F. Reynolds (c. 1818–?).

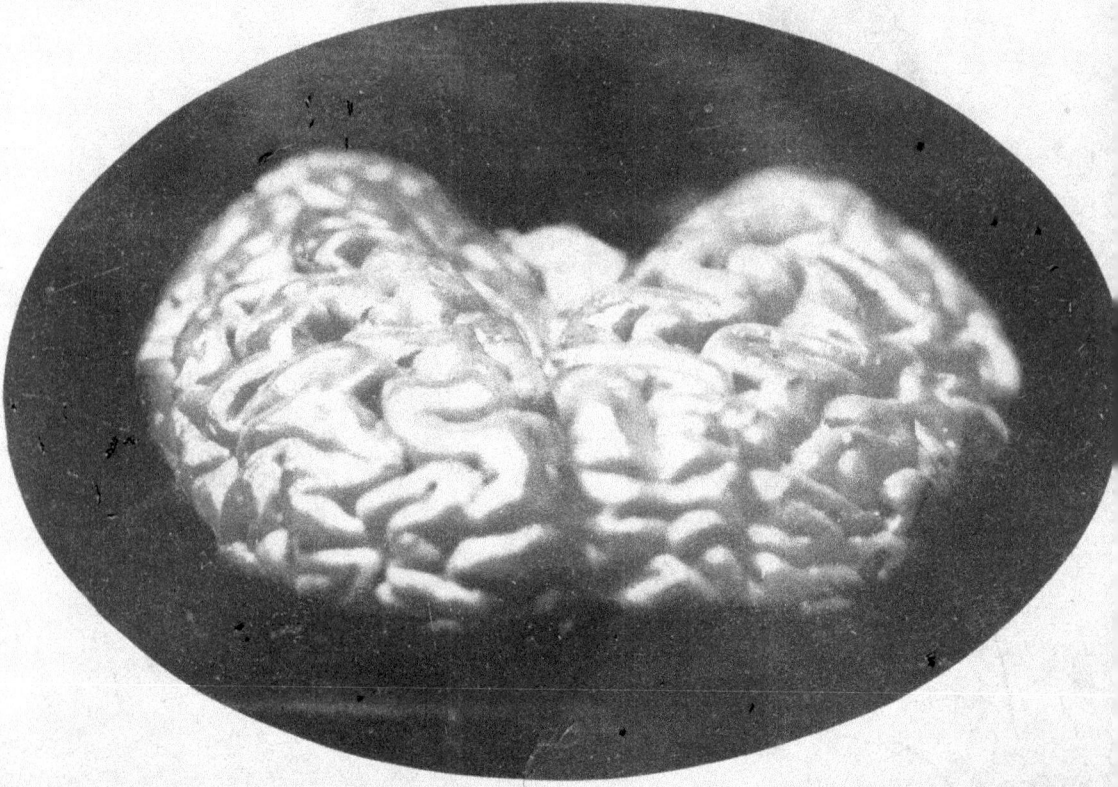

The brain of Charles Julius Guiteau (1841–1882), preserved as a specimen in the Mütter Museum, is part of the history of the insanity defense in the United States. Prosecuted for assassinating Pres. James A. Garfield, Guiteau (a former lawyer) represented himself during his trial, resting his defense on the assertion that he had been legally insane at the time he shot the president. Medical experts who testified (including fellows of The College of Physicians of Philadelphia) failed to agree on the defendant's sanity, and Guiteau was eventually convicted. After the execution, Guiteau's brain was autopsied in an effort to determine whether the state of his insanity could be determined by pathological signs, but no such signs were discovered.

In AD 46, Roman physician Scribonius Largus recommended that headaches be treated by applying living torpedo fish to the pain. Since a single fish discharges about 50 volts, it can be seen that this is one of the earliest documented medical prescriptions for electrotherapy. Medical applications of electricity gained much importance during the last half of the 19th century, with physicians using electrical treatments to try to restore nerve and muscle function for wounded Civil War soldiers. The electrical apparatus in this University of Pennsylvania laboratory was donated by Silas Weir Mitchell, MD, FCPP, a leading neurologist during and after the war. Electrical stimulation, along with bed rest, massage, and a high-calorie diet, was part of Mitchell's "rest cure" for depression. Today, physicians use electricity to restart stopped hearts, measure nerve and brain function, promote bone fusion, relieve pain, speed wound healing, and rehabilitate muscles.

Samuel David Gross (1805–1884), MD, FCPP, figures prominently in the development of surgery in the United States. Founder and president of the American Surgical Association, he was also president of the 1876 International Congress of Surgeons, the American Medical Association, the American Academy of Surgery, and the American Philosophical Society. His extensive library of surgical and medical books is housed at the library of The College of Physicians of Philadelphia. This portrait of Gross is by Italian artist T. Dimino (fl. 1909) and is probably a copy of the original portrait by Samuel Bell Waugh (1814–1855). One of the treasures of The College of Physicians of Philadelphia is Gross's engraved silver-hilted ceremonial sword.

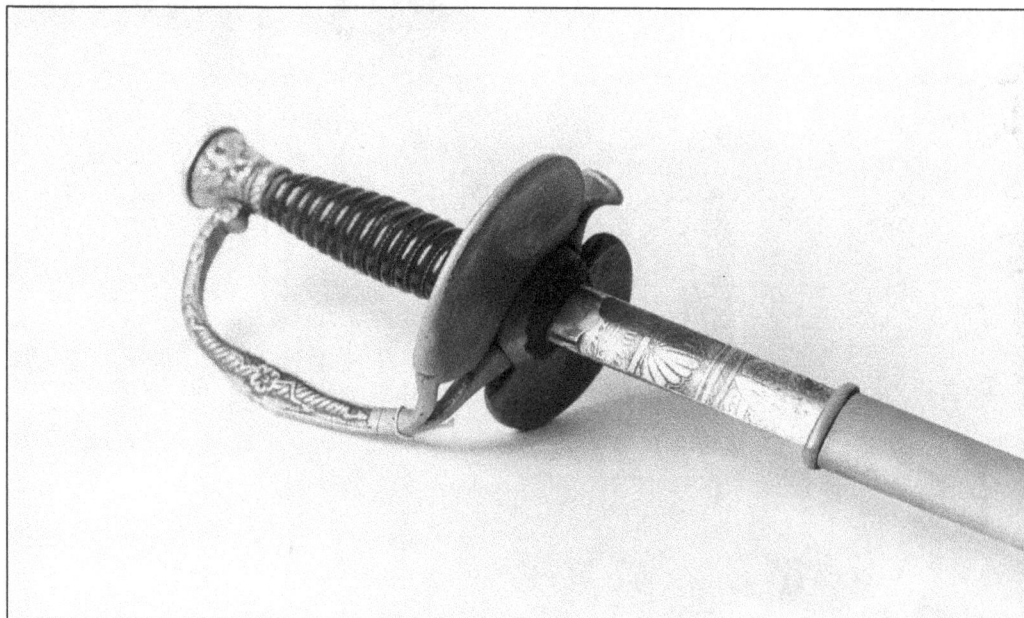

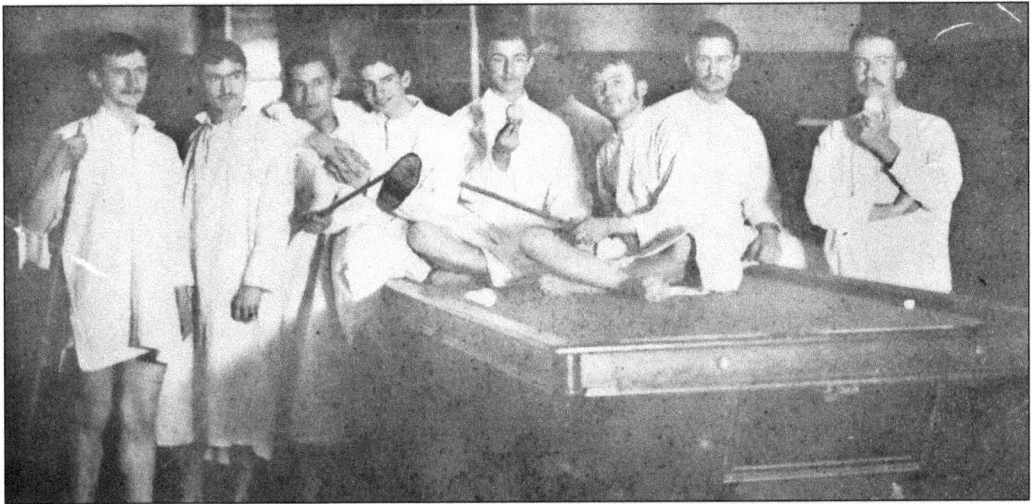

From playing billiards in the evening with other resident medical interns from the University of Pennsylvania in 1889, Joseph McFarland (1868–1945; fourth from left), MD, FCPP, went on to specialize in bacteriology, successfully developing vaccines for tetanus and diphtheria. He also contributed to this field with his development of the McFarland Turbidity Standards, which help medical researchers adjust bacterial suspensions for better accuracy. Elected a fellow of The College of Physicians of Philadelphia in 1895, he served as curator and honorary custodian of the Mütter Museum during the eight years before his death.

Following Boston Medical Library's first directory (1879), The College of Physicians of Philadelphia established the second directory of nurses in the United States in 1882. The purpose of the directory was to provide a reliable and comprehensive register of all local qualified nurses. By the end of 1882, the college's directory registered 187 qualified nurses for the Philadelphia area. This directory was a great help to physicians in providing nursing care for their patients.

William W. Keen (1837–1932), MD, FCPP, served as surgeon to the Fifth Massachusetts Regiment during the Civil War before being commissioned by the US Army to run military hospitals in Washington, DC, and Philadelphia. A brilliant teacher, researcher, and surgeon, he was responsible for many medical firsts. He was the first surgeon in Philadelphia to use Lister's methods for antiseptic surgery. He performed the first successful operations in the United States to remove a brain tumor and to correct microcephaly (a condition in which the skull fails to grow at the same rate as the rest of the face and head). He also served as president of The College of Physicians of Philadelphia from 1900 to 1901.

During a heated debate in 1893 over the repeal of silver coinage, Pres. Grover Cleveland was diagnosed with a tumor in his mouth. Wishing to maintain the appearance of good health in the midst of this public crisis, the president chose to have the tumor removed in a secret operation. Taken a few days after the operation, this cast of Cleveland's upper palate shows the extent of the surgical excision. Several months later, a new cast showed that Cleveland's mouth had healed well. The secret operation was revealed to the public in 1917 by Keen, one of the physicians who had performed the surgery. The tumor itself (preserved as a specimen in the Mütter Museum) was analyzed in 1980 and determined to be a malignant cancer. The secret operation had saved the president's life.

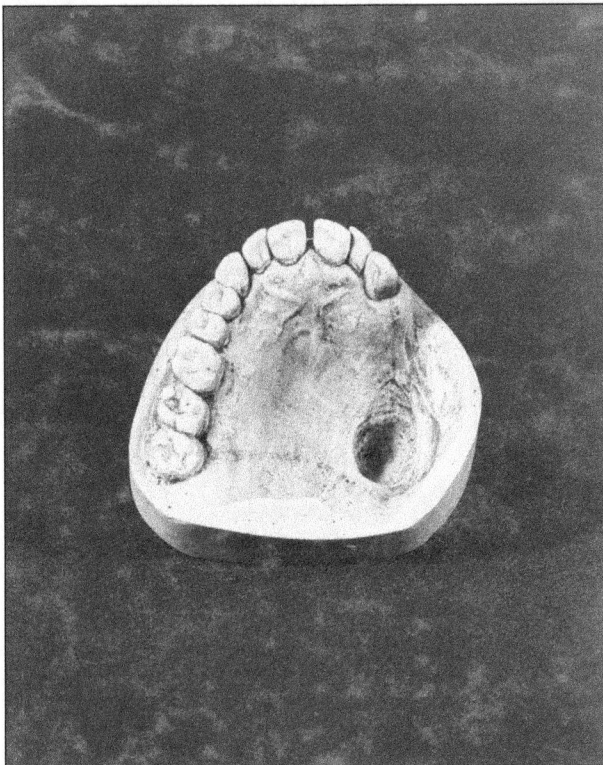

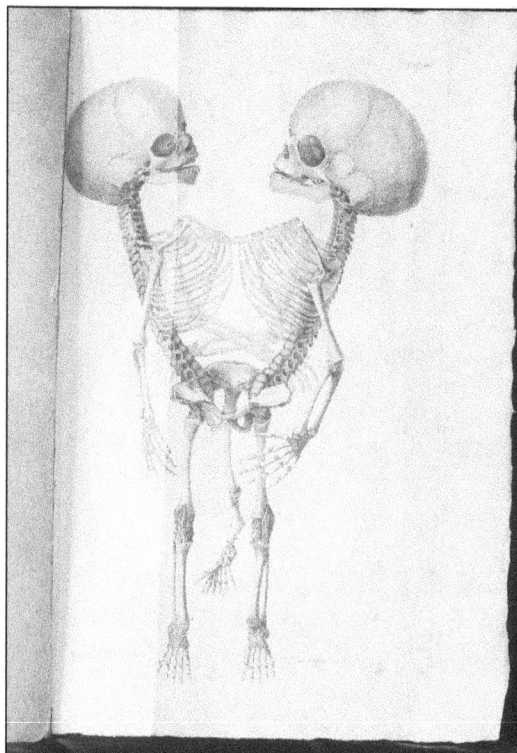

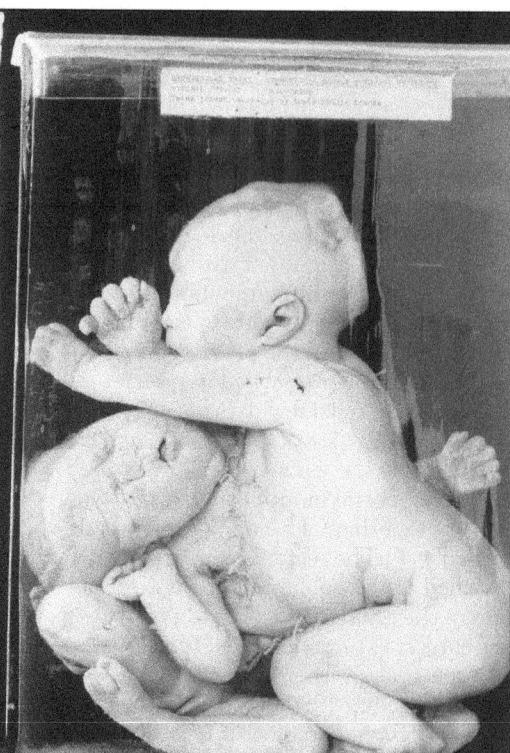

Infants whose bodies are physically joined at some point on their bodies are called conjoined twins. C. Everett Koop (b. 1916), MD, FCPP, surgeon general of the United States from 1982 to 1989, developed groundbreaking surgical procedures for separating conjoined twins. He gained international recognition in 1957 through his successful separation of twins conjoined at the buttocks and again in 1974 through his separation of twins conjoined at the spine who shared a liver, colon, and intestines. His pioneering techniques are now commonly used by other surgeons and have saved the lives of hundreds of infants. (AB conjoined twins.)

Six

DURING WAR

Pvt. John Brooks, Company I, 57th Pennsylvania Volunteers, shows the result of a fracture of the temporal bone by a musket ball. Brooks, 17 years old, was wounded at the Battle of the Wilderness in Virginia, May 1864. The wound was large enough to admit the introduction of two fingers into the cavity, but his brain was not injured. After several surgeries, Brooks was discharged from the service fully recovered.

William Fisher Norris (1839–1901, top center), MD, FCPP, an assistant surgeon and captain in the Union army, was appointed director of Douglas Hospital in Washington, DC, in 1864. He appears here in front of the hospital with his medical staff. After the war, he became one of the first physicians to use photography to record the appearance of diseases and wounds.

This field hospital report was written by William Henry Dickerson, a major and surgeon in the Confederate army. Dated 20 days after the Union victory at the Siege of Vicksburg in 1863, the report displays the overwhelming rate of disease among Civil War soldiers. Of Dickerson's 93 patients on July 24, only one was wounded. Malaria, dysentery, typhoid fever, pneumonia, tuberculosis, and other diseases devastated both armies during that war.

Turner's Lane Hospital in Philadelphia was a 400-bed hospital specializing in the care of Civil War soldiers with nervous disorders. As America's first neurological research hospital, Turner's Lane produced important data that led to the diagnosis and treatment of what is now call posttraumatic stress disorder. But Turner's Lane was only one of 24 military hospitals in Philadelphia during the Civil War. The two largest military hospitals in the United States were both in Philadelphia: Mower (3,600 beds and 20,000 patients during the war) and Satterlee (4,500 beds and 12,000 patients during the war). An estimated 157,000 Civil War soldiers and sailors were treated in Philadelphia's hospitals.

David Hayes Agnew (1818–1892), MD, FCPP, was an exceptional surgeon and professor of anatomy. A prolific author of medical textbooks and an outstanding lecturer, Agnew was popular with his students. In gratitude for his exceptional teaching, they commissioned the celebrated artist Thomas Eakins to paint his largest work, *The Agnew Clinic*. At the request of the commissioners, Eakins carved a Latin inscription into the frame. Translated, this inscription praises Agnew as "the most experienced surgeon, the clearest writer and teacher, the most venerated and beloved man." During the Civil War, Agnew treated soldiers in one of the Union army's largest military hospitals, Mower US Army General Hospital in Philadelphia. Here, he acquired a national reputation for his expertise in treating gunshot wounds and accordingly was appointed chief consulting surgeon to President Garfield after the latter was mortally wounded by an assassin's bullet.

Jacob Mendez Da Costa (1833–1900), MD, FCPP, treated Civil War soldiers at Turner's Lane Hospital. Here, he undertook the first clinical research on "soldier's heart," a condition then thought to be a form of heart disease. Da Costa's landmark study linked this condition, common in soldiers during times of war, to an anxiety disorder that is now known as Da Costa's syndrome.

Joseph Leidy (1823–1891), MD, FCPP, served as a surgeon during the Civil War. A pioneering parasitologist, Leidy was one of the first to realize that trichinosis is caused by eating parasite-infested meat. In 1846, he became the first person to use a microscope to solve a homicide. The accused claimed that the blood on his clothes was from a chicken, but Leidy demonstrated that the blood was human.

Pvt. John Schranz, 7th Austrian Feldjägers, was wounded in the left thigh in May 1859. Surgeons first removed the upper part of the thigh bone and later the entire limb. By January 1860, Schranz was described as "in excellent condition" and walking with the aid of a crutch.

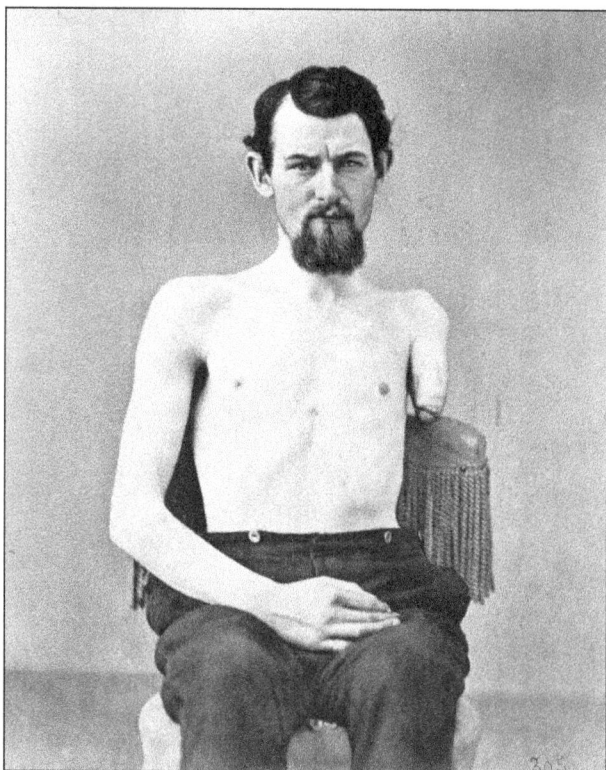

Cpl. J.B. Joyce, Company I, 7th Vermont Volunteers, was injured by a cannon explosion at Barrancas, Florida, in 1863. Joyce's left arm was amputated above the elbow, but the wound became gangrenous, and Joyce himself extracted a three-inch piece of bone. He was working as a clerk in the Paymaster General's Office when this photograph was taken in 1871.

Sometimes military surgeons had great success treating their patients and were able to restore them to excellent condition. Pvt. John Brink, Company K, 11th Pennsylvania Cavalry, was injured by a guerilla band during a scouting expedition near Windsor, Virginia, and was taken to a regimental hospital immediately. Surgeons removed the upper part of his right upper arm bone. By the time of his discharge, Brink could move his shoulder through a wide range of motion, and his hand and forearm were unimpaired. Pvt. W.F. Ford, Company K, 8th Ohio Volunteers, was wounded by a ramrod in the thigh at Antietam, Maryland, in 1862. The wound resulted in stiffness of the joint, which made Ford slightly lame, but his overall health was reported as good. In the photograph, the presence of the mirror makes it possible to see both the entrance and exit wounds.

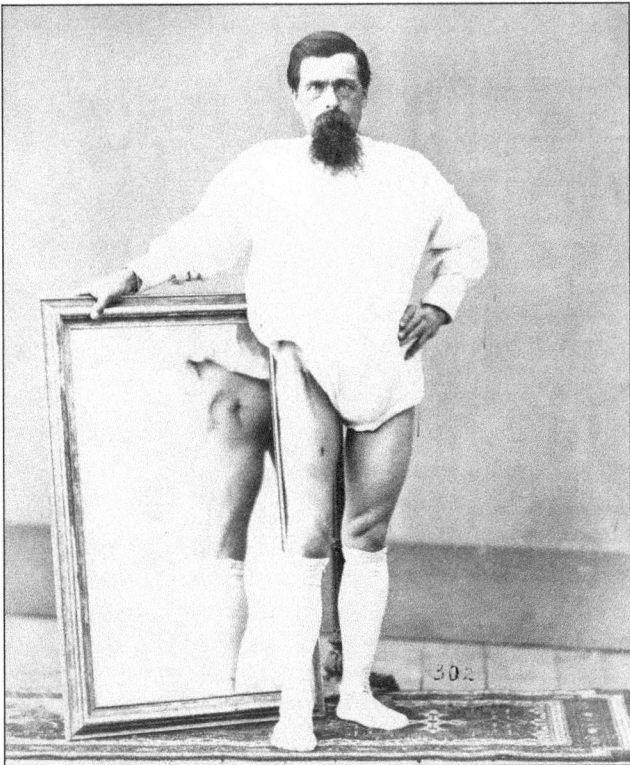

Medical ambulances, one of the innovations of Jonathan Letterman, MD, first appeared as horse-drawn wagons to retrieve wounded soldiers from Civil War battlefields. Before ambulances, wounded soldiers had lain on battlefields for days without water, food, or medical attention. Letterman's ambulances, however, insured that all 23,000 soldiers wounded at the Battle of Antietam in 1862 were removed to safety and medical assistance within 24 hours.

This c. 1888 image from Old Blockley is labeled "Men of the out wards." Seriously ill patients were assigned to "in wards" inside the main hospital building, easily accessible by hospital staff. Other patients were assigned to "out wards" (separate dormitories) in smaller buildings apart from the main hospital. The date of this photograph indicates that these men were probably veterans of the Civil War.

Astley Paston Cooper Ashhurst (1876–1932, right), MD, FCPP, poses with fellow physicians in 1916 at military training camp in Plattsburg, New York. Ashhurst served during World War I as director of US Base Hospital 34 in Nantes, France, and as chief surgeon at Walter Reed Army Medical Center near Washington, DC, before his honorable discharge in 1919.

George William Norris (1875–1965), MD, FCPP, son of Civil War surgeon William Fisher Norris, served as a US Army colonel at British Hospital No. 16 in Le Treport, France, during World War I. He also acted as medical consultant in the Toul Sector, participating in the Saint Mihiel offensive. General Pershing cited Norris for "exceptionally meritorious and conspicuous services."

During the Civil War, a horse-drawn wagon for conveying wounded soldiers off the field of battle was called a mobile hospital or *hôpital ambulant* (French for "walking hospital"). By World War I, these conveyances were powered by internal combustion engines rather than horses. To aid the war effort, wealthy families donated their personal automobiles to be fitted with ambulance bodies. Some of these families also volunteered their household chauffeurs to serve as ambulance drivers. Manufacturers of ambulances included Rolls-Royce, Daimler, Morris, Austin, Renault, Buick, Fiat, and Ford (Model T). The ambulances in these photographs were used at US Base Hospital 34 in Nantes, France, directed by Astley Paston Cooper Ashhurst, MD, FCPP.

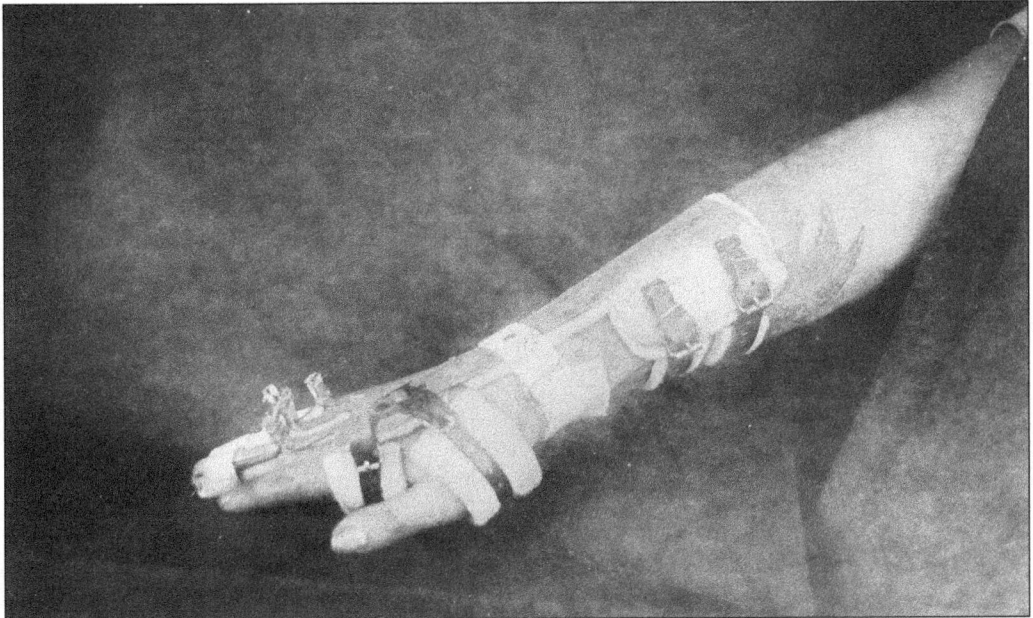

The immobilization of injured limbs by splinting is a centuries-old medical practice, but 20th-century technological advances in the production of metal supports and fasteners rendered the use of splints quicker and easier than before. One benefit of splinting is that it diminishes pain and reduces internal bleeding, thus reducing the risk of shock to the patient. Another benefit is that splinting prevents broken bones from piercing the skin and opening the body to infection. (When this occurred, the affected limb had to be amputated to prevent the patient from dying of sepsis.) A third benefit is that splinting aligns the bone for proper healing. Efficient and practical splinting on the large scale demanded in wartime was developed during World War I, reducing mortality from certain fractures resulting from bullet and shrapnel wounds from 80 percent to less than 10 percent.

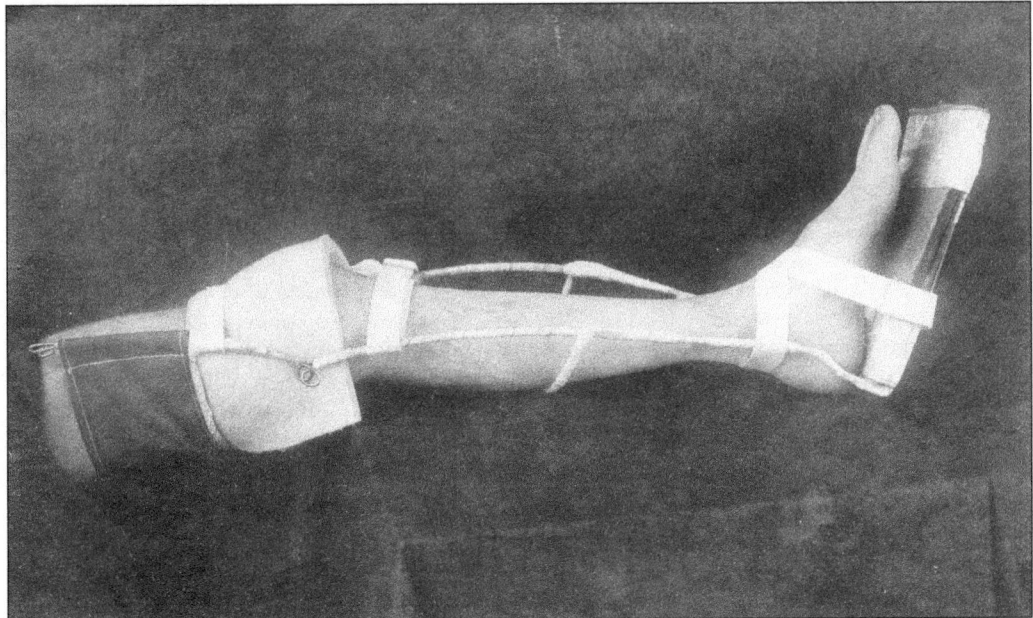

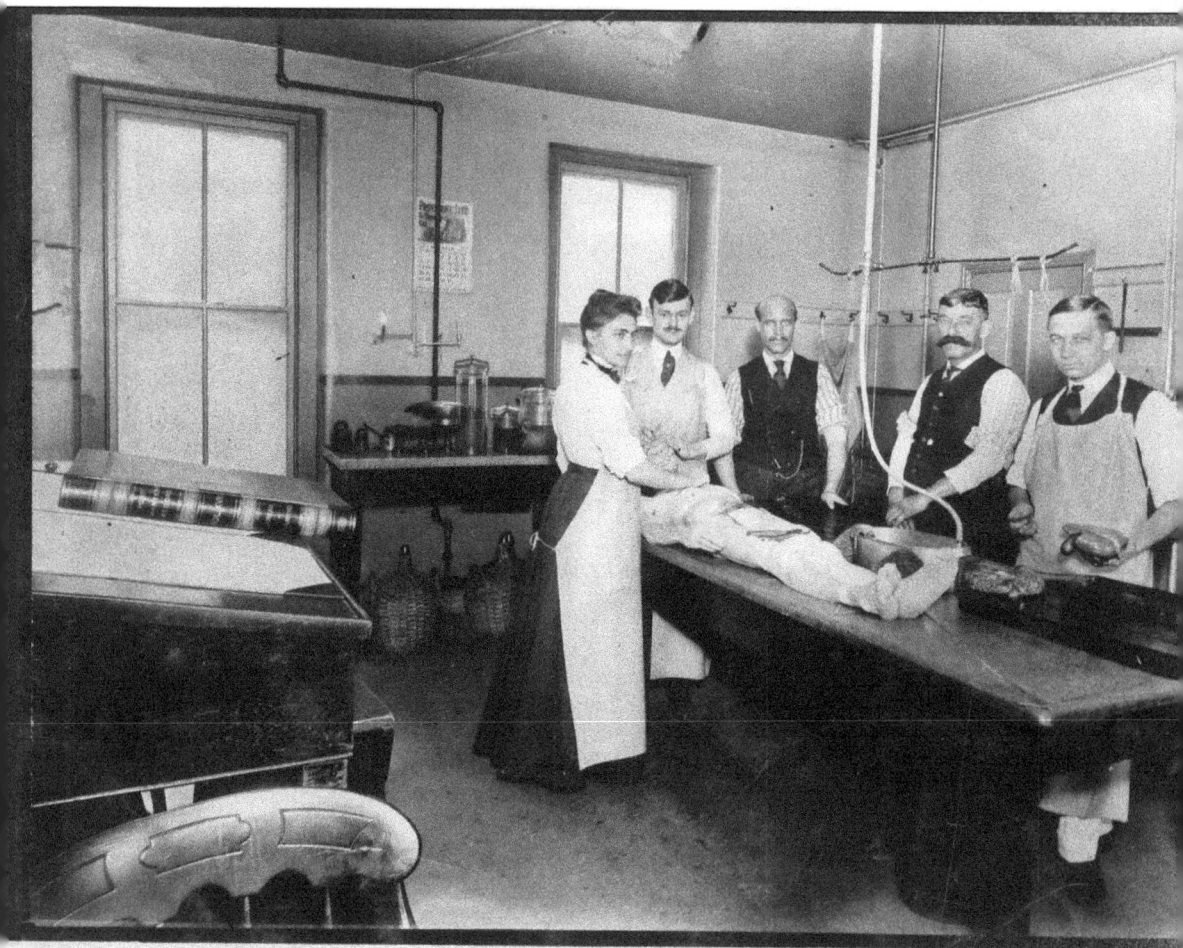

1903

James Douglas Blackwood (1881–1942, right), MD, served as a physician during both World War I and World War II. He earned the Navy Cross for tending to the wounded when the troop transport USS *President Lincoln* was torpedoed in 1918. He also served as a public health officer during the American occupation of Haiti (1915–1934) and as a medical inspector during World War II. During the Battle of Savo Island, part of the Solomon Islands campaign of 1942, he died when the Japanese sank four ships including his, the USS *Vincennes*. In his honor, the destroyer escort USS *J. Douglas Blackwood* was commissioned in 1943.

92

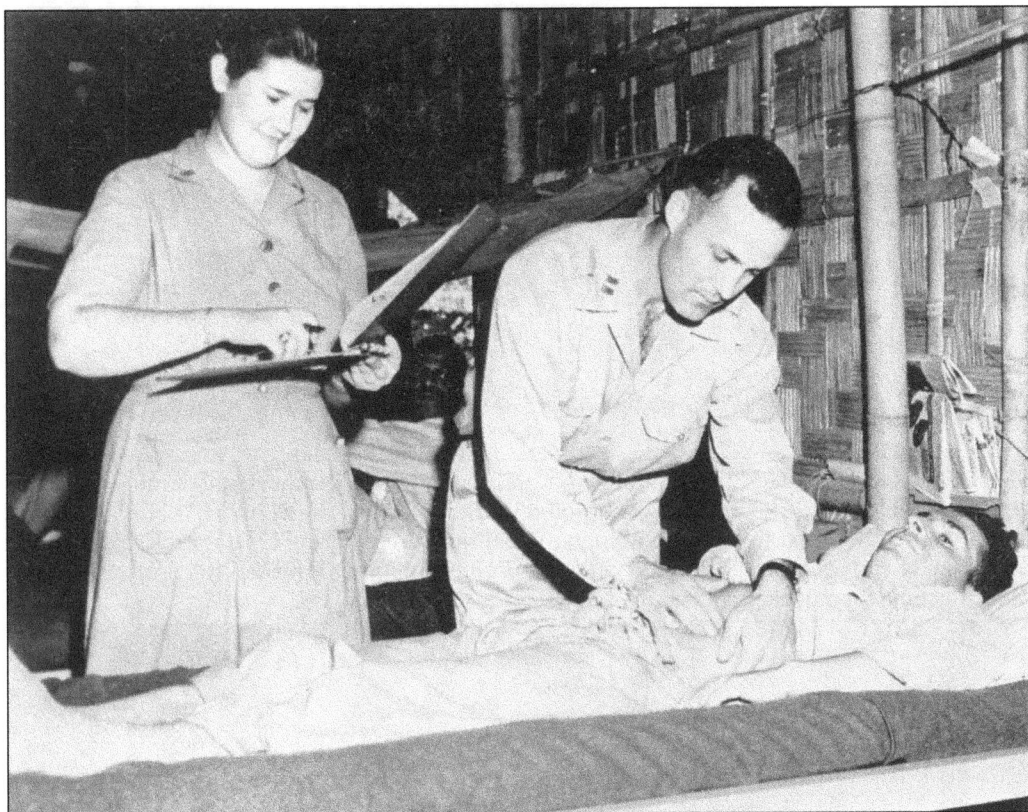

Near the end of World War II, the military system of portable surgical hospitals, field hospitals, and general hospitals was supplemented by a new development: the mobile army surgical hospital (MASH). These MASH units were designed to move medical staff closer to the front lines in order to expedite the treatment of wounded soldiers. Emergency surgery was first performed at a battalion aid station, and then casualties were routed to the MASH unit for more extensive treatment. This system worked very well; during the Korean War, a seriously wounded soldier who underwent treatment in a MASH unit had a 97 percent chance of survival.

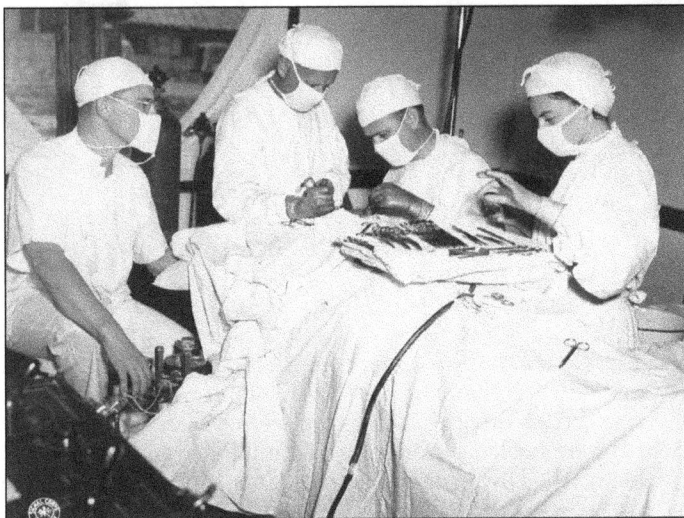

MASH units saved soldiers' lives not only in Korea, but also in Vietnam, Saudi Arabia, Iraq, and elsewhere. The most decorated combat hospital in the US Army, the 212th MASH, was the first military hospital established in Iraq to support coalition forces during Operation Iraqi Freedom. Two years later, the United States donated the entire hospital to Pakistan to contribute to the 2005 Kashmir earthquake relief effort.

Female nurses have served in every military conflict involving the United States. Hundreds were wounded and died of infectious diseases such as typhoid fever. Some of the 12,000 nurses who served in World War II were held as prisoners of war and killed in escape attempts. Many have received medals, including the Distinguished Service Cross, an award second only to the Medal of Honor.

94

Seven

THE MÜTTER MUSEUM

Thomas Dent Mütter (1811–1859), MD, FCPP, a pioneering plastic surgeon renowned for his work in repairing club feet and cleft palates, endowed the medical museum that now bears his name and bequeathed his collection of medical specimens to it. Even today, a century and a half after its founding, the museum still exhibits many of Mütter's original specimens, such as the wax model of Madame Sunday. This oil portrait of Mütter was created by Daniel Huntington (1816–1906).

Added to the small collection of specimens already held by the college, Mütter's generous donation created a nationally significant museum. Under the curatorship of Thomas Hewson Bache (1826–1912), MD, FCPP, the museum acquired such important material as the magnificent collection of delicate eardrums prepared by renowned otologist Adam Politzer (1835–1920), MD. Another important specimen is the "soap lady," a naturally preserved body from the 1830s that offers medical researchers a rare opportunity for study. Originally obtained for the museum in 1875 at a cost of $7.50, the soap lady is now considered priceless. A recent significant acquisition is a collection of beautifully prepared slides of portions of Albert Einstein's brain. These slides were donated by neuropathologist Lucy Rorke-Adams, MD, FCPP. Rorke-Adams believes that future study of these slides may reveal significant new findings regarding the connection between human intelligence and the structure of the brain.

Gretchen Worden (1947–2004) worked at the Mütter Museum for nearly 30 years, moving up from assistant curator to museum director. Not only did she expand the museum's holdings, she greatly increased public attendance. She appeared frequently on television and radio to speak about the museum, invited photographers and other artists to use the museum's collections as inspiration for their work, and increased museum revenue through the publication of books and calendars featuring photographs of museum specimens. Worden encouraged museum visitors to rethink their definitions of what it means to be human: "While these bodies may be ugly," she wrote of the specimens in the museum, "there is a terrifying beauty in the spirits of those forced to endure these afflictions." Worden transformed the museum from a collection of oddities practically unknown to the general public into one of Philadelphia's most popular cultural institutions. Now it is known throughout the world.

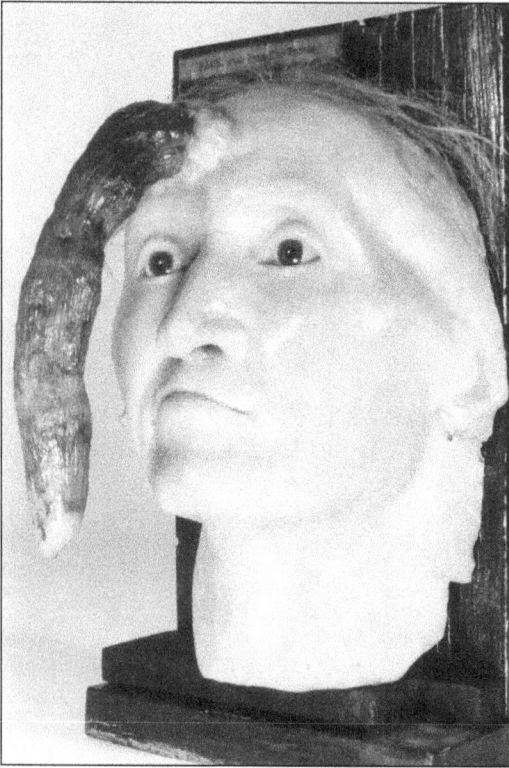

A skin horn is a growth formed from the material that makes up human skin and hair. This growth resembles a horn but contains no bone, as a true horn does. One of the best known cutaneous horns belonged to a Parisian widow surnamed Dimanche (c. 1756–c. 1839), whose 10-inch horn protruded from her forehead. This wax model of Madame Dimanche (Madame Sunday) is one of the museum's most popular exhibits.

Wax models have been of great educational value to medical science for centuries. More detailed and lifelike than two-dimensional drawings or photographs, models allow physicians and medical students to visualize the effects that disease has on the human body. Wax simulates human skin in its translucent surface and tendency to secrete moisture. (AB.)

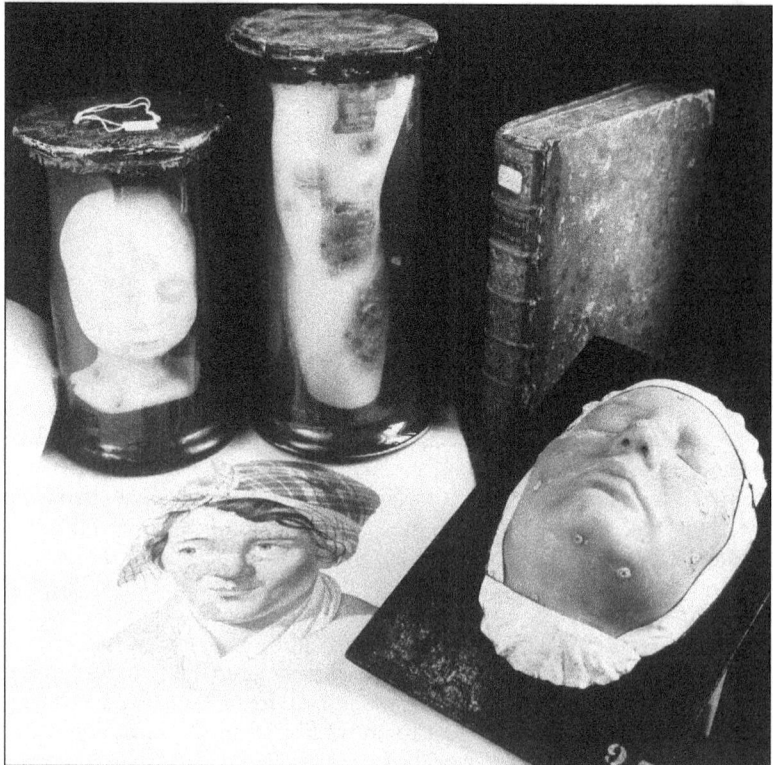

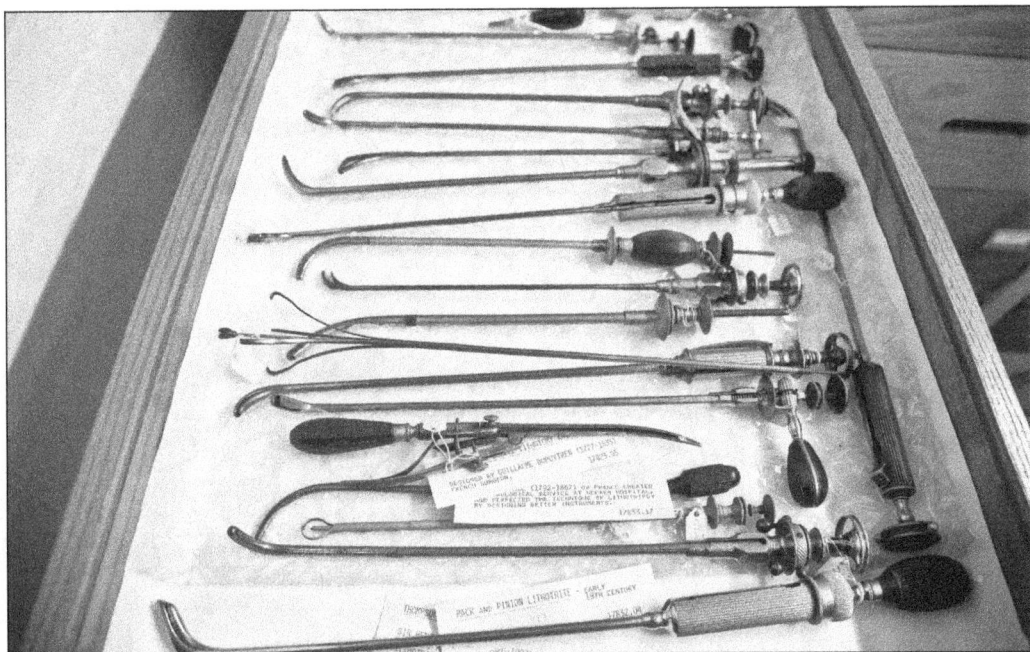

For at least 7,000 years, surgeons cut open a living human body in order to remove stones that had formed inside a hollow organ, such as the kidney, bladder, or gallbladder. The instrument used to perform this removal was a lithotrite. The lithotrites in the museum's collection display a wide range of designs. Today, such stones are crushed while inside the body and excreted naturally. (AB.)

From the mid-19th to the mid-20th century, electrotherapy devices became increasingly popular among medical practitioners. Static electric machines (an early one was invented by Benjamin Franklin), Galvanic and Faradic batteries, Tesla and induction coils, ultraviolet rays, diathermy machines, carbon arc lamps, magneto-electric machines such as the one in this photograph, and other devices were perceived (sometimes wrongly) as having medical applications.

Among the museum's hundreds of skulls is a very special collection assembled by one of the world's greatest teachers of anatomy, Josef Hyrtl (1810–1894). Unlike most preserved skulls, which were saved because they belonged to celebrities or criminals, Hyrtl's collection consists of the skulls of ordinary people, each skull labeled with facts about the original owner. Julius Farkas, age 28, a Protestant soldier, committed suicide by a gunshot wound to the heart because of "weariness of life." Geza Uirmeny, a Hungarian or Romanian herdsman, survived a suicide attempt at age 70 and lived 10 more years "without melancholy."

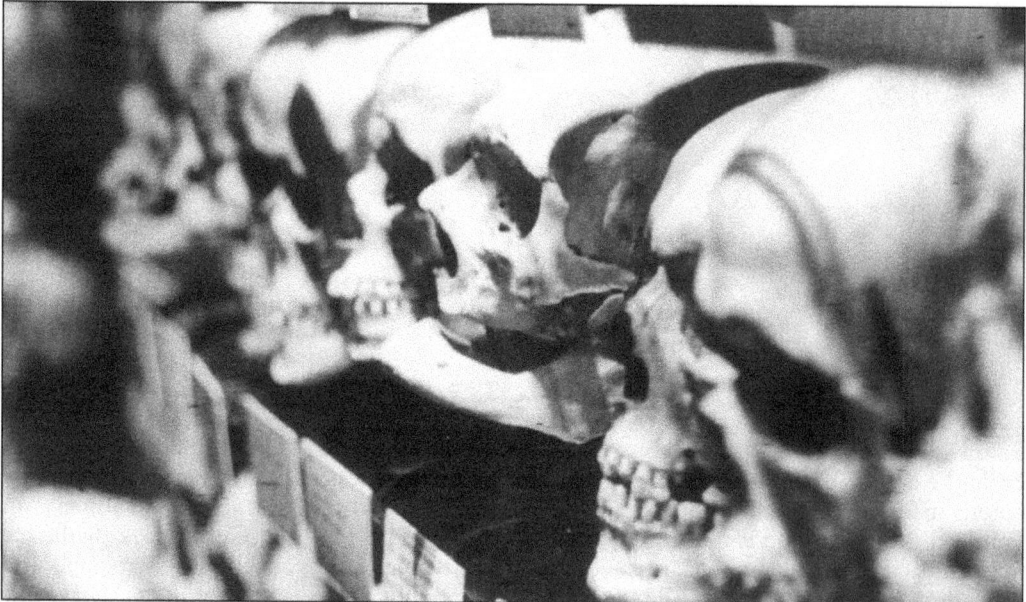

Most conjoined twins are fused at the chest, belly, or both. Less common joinings involve fusion at the face, spine, or pelvis. This skeleton is from a pair of twins who were fused at both the head and the thorax. Conjoined twins have been documented for at least 2,000 years, but successful surgical separation was accomplished only during the 20th century. Because the life of one twin is often jeopardized by separation surgery, the ethics of separation are complex. Some twins prefer to remain fused. The quality of life for conjoined twins varies considerably depending on the site of the fusion and the involvement of internal organs. Many conjoined twins have lived productive lives, such as Chang and Eng Bunker. Lori and George Schappell (b. 1961) are conjoined twins who attended college, appear frequently on television, and maintain separate personal and public lives. George is an award-winning country singer, while Lori is a trophy-winning bowler.

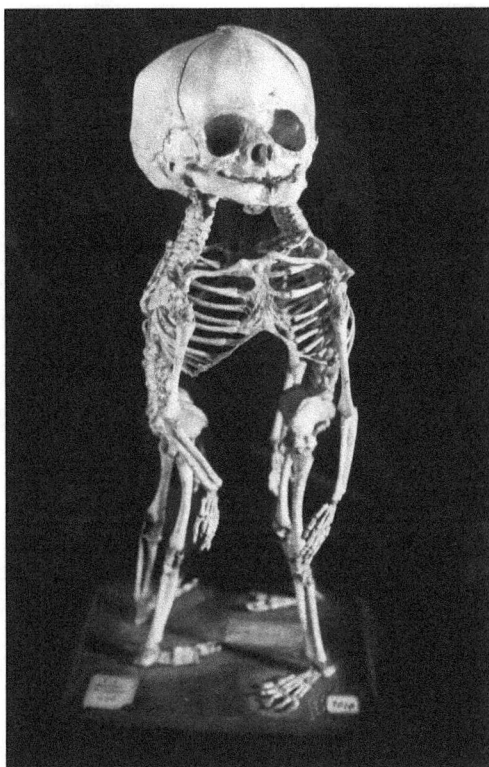

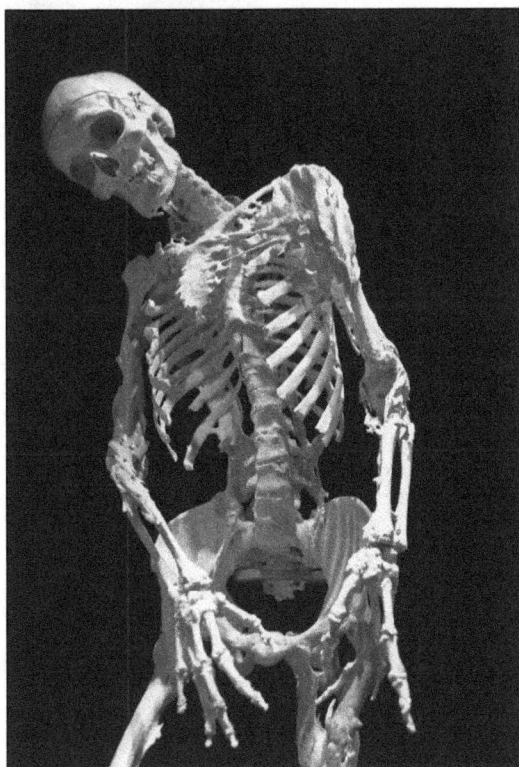

Harry R. Eastlack, Jr. (1933–1973) suffered from fibrodysplasia ossificans progressiva (FOP), a disease in which the body's bone-repair mechanism malfunctions, changing muscles and tendons into bone. After an initial injury at age 10, Eastlack's body began to turn to bone and continued to do so with every bump he suffered. His willingness to allow his skeleton to be studied by researchers assisted the discovery in 2006 of the one gene mutation in six billion that is responsible for the excessive growth of bone in FOP. This groundbreaking discovery—made by a team headed by Frederick S. Kaplan, MD, FCPP—will be instrumental in the development of a cure for FOP. It will also assist researchers and physicians in developing better treatments for osteoporosis, osteoarthritis, postamputation treatment, complications following hip replacements, spinal cord injuries, head injuries, and heart valve disorders. Thus one person's donation of his or her body to medical research can improve the lives of millions of other people.

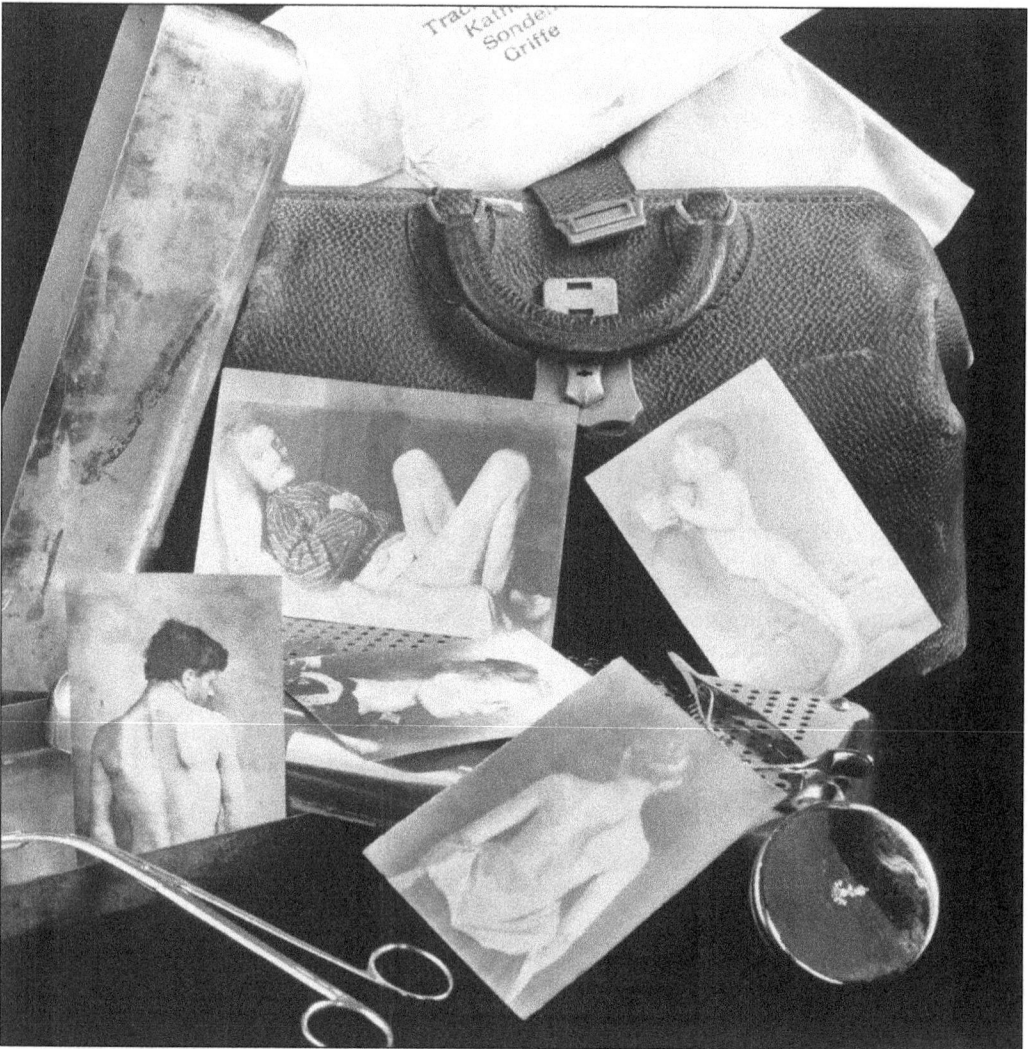

Medical photographs began to appear in the 1840s, but not until the Civil War did the true value of photography in medicine become apparent. Hundreds of photographs of injuries from this war are now preserved at The College of Physicians of Philadelphia. Technological developments that added new dimensions to medical photography included stereoscopic photography, endoscopic photography, microphotography, and motion studies. The latter began when Eadweard Muybridge (1830–1904) created motion studies of people performing routine actions such as hopping and walking upstairs. Muybridge's work inspired others to apply his principles to medical photography. French physician Étienne-Jules Marey (1830–1904) studied human motion through serial photographic studies and devised the first motion picture camera. By the end of the 19th century, medical applications of all types of photography were routine. (AB.)

One of medical photography's great values lies in teaching the clinical signs of disease to students. This photograph shows a man with greatly swollen feet, ankles, and lower legs. These symptoms indicate a disease called elephantiasis (often wrongly pronounced "elephantitis," which means "inflammation of the elephant"). One type of elephantiasis occurs when tiny worms enter the human body after mosquitoes break the skin. The worms cause the swelling by blocking lymph vessels.

Case of T. G. Morton M.D

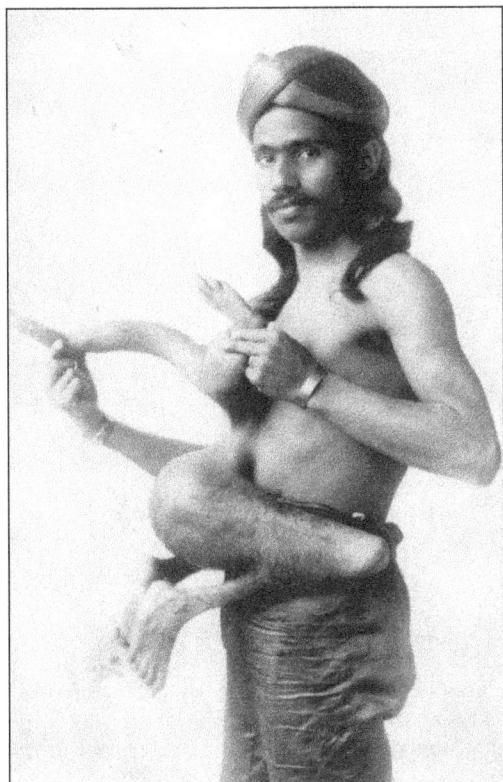

Perumal Sami (1888–after 1915) publicly exhibited his parasitic twin at several venues, including the 1904 Saint Louis World's Fair. Parasitic twinning occurs when conjoined embryos fail to separate in the womb, and one twin continues to develop while the other does not. Perumal Sami and his brother illustrate a condition in which the parasitic twin fails to develop a head and heart, instead relying for its blood supply on its sibling.

103

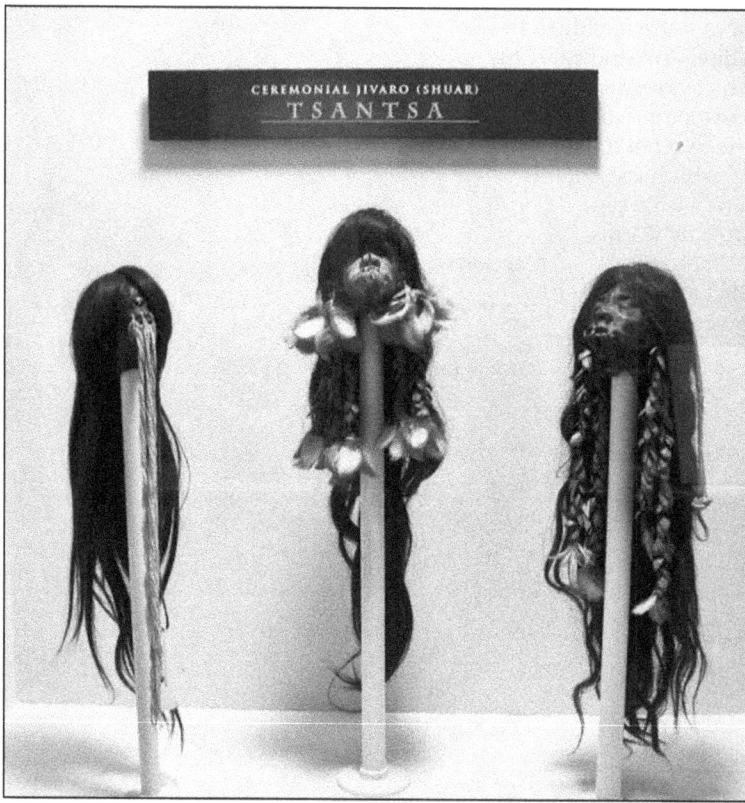

CEREMONIAL JIVARO (SHUAR)
TSANTSA

Most of the museum's anatomical specimens pertain to medical study, but some relate more to anthropology. The collection of *tsantsa*—shrunken human heads—is an example of anatomical specimens produced originally for religious reasons rather than medical ones. For many centuries, the Jívaro people (particularly the Shuar subgroup) of the Ecuadorian-Peruvian Amazon Basin decapitated their enemies in order to shrink their heads, thus controlling the vengeful spirits of the dead.

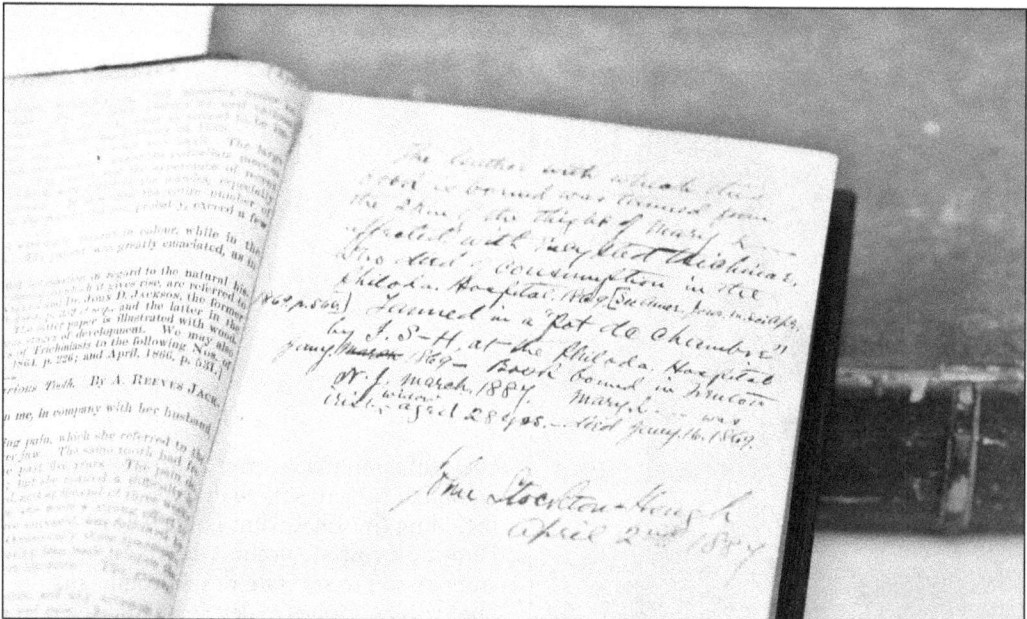

Binding books in human skin—anthropodermic bibliopegy—has occasionally been practiced by doctors as a way of honoring special patients. This inscription, which was written by John Stockton-Hough, MD, states that this book is bound in the skin of a patient who died of trichinosis in 1869. Stockton-Hough tanned the skin himself at Philadelphia Hospital.

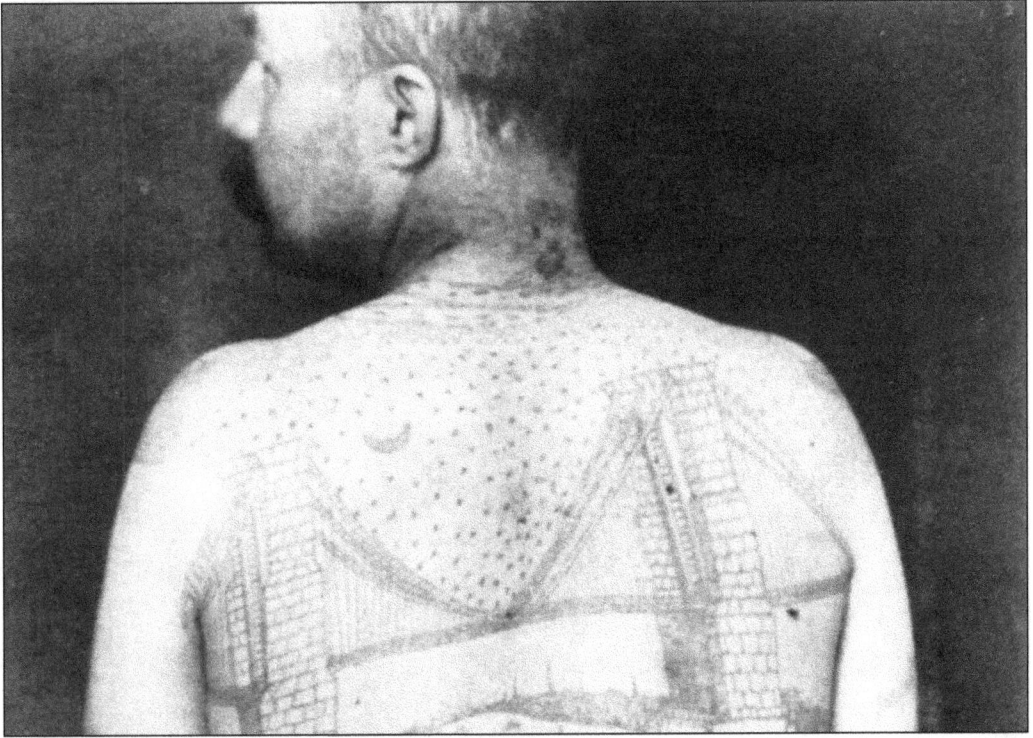

Humans have tattooed themselves for more than 6,000 years. Most tattoos serve art rather than medicine (such as this mid-20th-century photograph of a man tattooed with the Brooklyn Bridge), but tattooing also has medical applications. For instance, a person with a medical condition such as heart disease, epilepsy, or diabetes may choose to wear a tattoo that notifies others of this condition rather than wearing a medical alert bracelet or pendant.

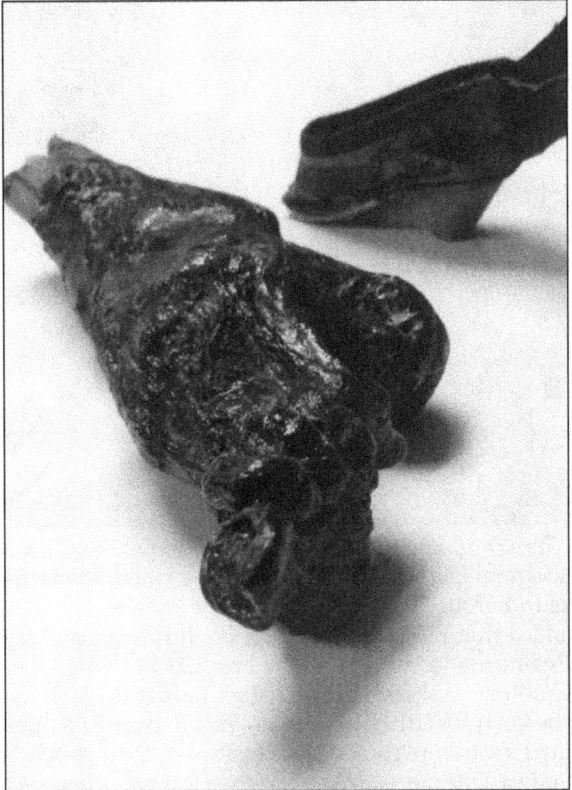

This specimen of a Chinese woman's bound foot, accompanied by its three-inch-long slipper, demonstrates anatomical modification. The bones were broken to allow the foot to fold in half at the instep and the toes to be permanently wrapped under the foot. This type of modification is of interest to physicians because it demonstrates the possibilities and limitations of the healing capabilities of the human body.

Chang and Eng Bunker (1811–1874) were born joined from the navel to the lower breastbone. As adolescents, they earned money by exhibiting themselves in North and South America as well as in Europe. They became so well known that their public promotion as the "Siamese twins" added that phrase to common English usage and is now used to describe any conjoined twins. Beginning in the 1830s, the brothers became American citizens, plantation owners in North Carolina, husbands to two sisters, fathers to 21 children, and slave owners. Financially ruined by the Civil War, they were again forced to go on exhibition tours to support their families. Popular myths attribute their deaths in 1874 to toxic shock, stroke, pneumonia, heart failure, blood loss, and various other causes, but the facts are otherwise.

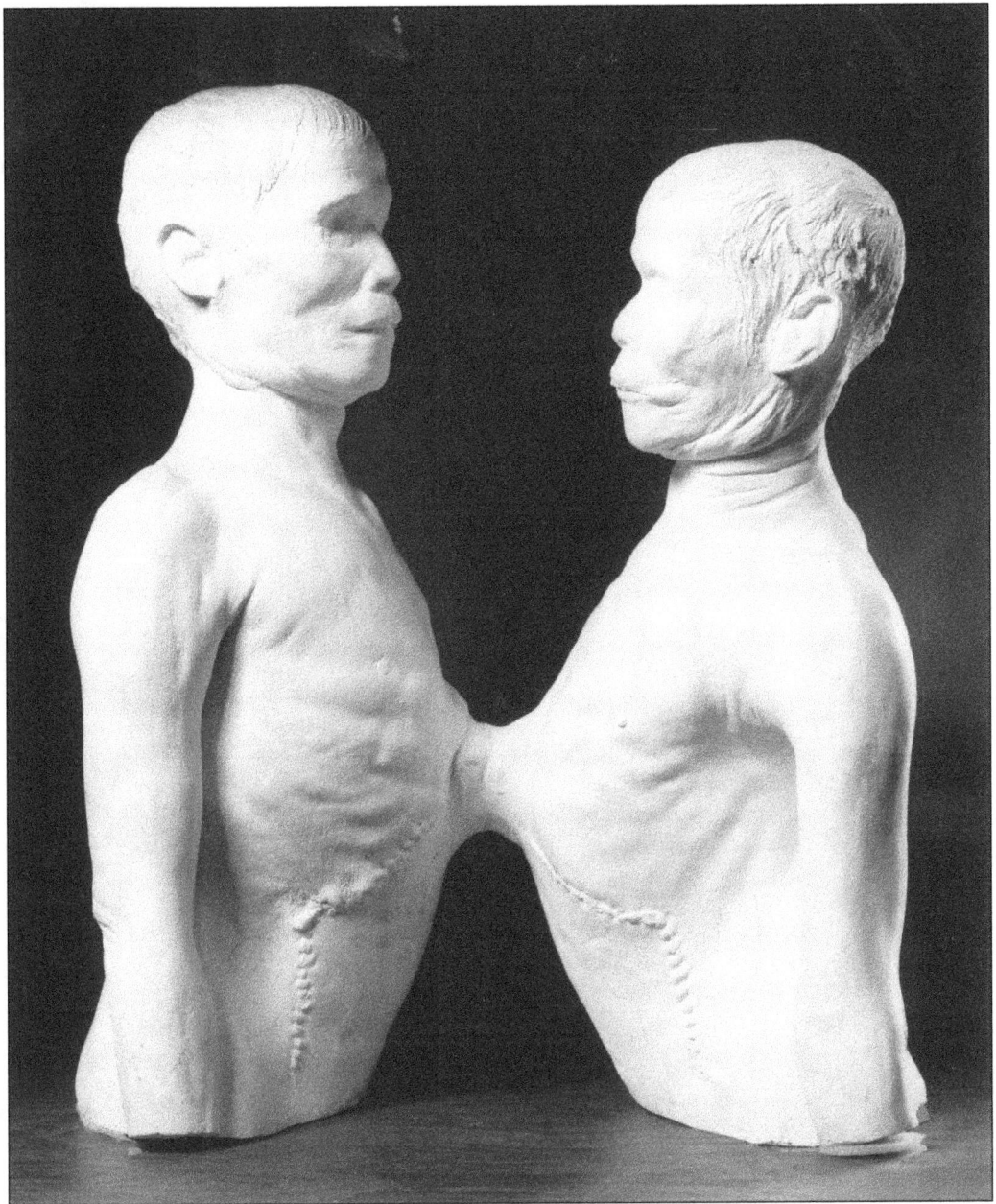

The bodies of the Bunker brothers were separated and autopsied at The College of Physicians of Philadelphia by William Henry Pancoast, MD, FCPP, and Harrison Allen, MD, FCPP. According to Allen's autopsy report, "[I]n consequence of the restrictions by which we were bound, no examination of the brains was made. It cannot, therefore, be proved that the cause of Chang's death was a cerebral clot, although such an opinion, from the suddenness of death, preceded as it was by hemiplegia and an immediate engorgement of the left lung, is tenable. Eng died, in all probability, in a state of syncope induced by fright—a view which the over-distended bladder and the retraction of the right testicle would appear to corroborate." The Mütter Museum contains a plaster death cast of the Bunker twins' torsos before the separation, their actual conjoined livers preserved as a specimen, and photographs of the autopsy.

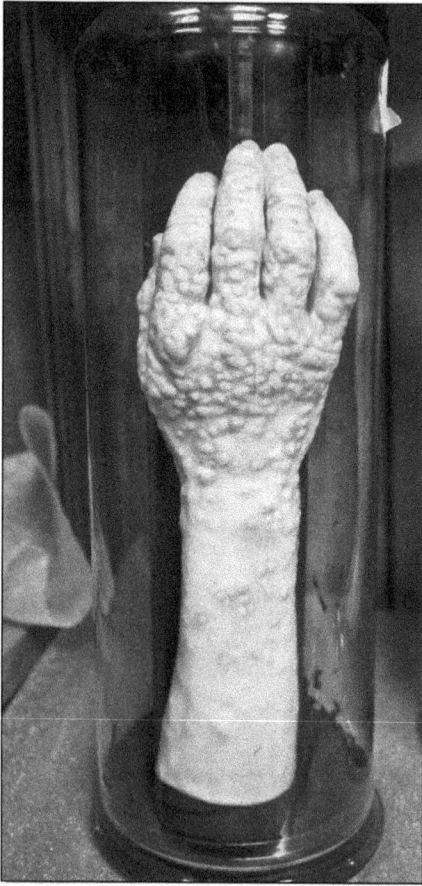

This wax model of an adult arm shows the clinical signs of smallpox, which killed 300–500 million people during the first eight decades of the 20th century. International vaccination campaigns during the 19th and 20th centuries helped eradicate smallpox from the world in 1979—one of medical science's greatest triumphs. The United States stopped vaccinating the general population in 1972 and military recruits in 1990.

Gunshot wounds cause serious physical trauma to the human body. Photographs of gunshot wounds from the 19th and early 20th centuries are valuable because they help medical professionals better understand injuries inflicted by improvised (unconventional) firearms. This man's misaligned left leg resulted from a bullet to the knee.

Eight

ART AND TREASURES

The College of Physicians of Philadelphia's art collection includes paintings, sculptures, drawings, and photographs. The crown jewel of this collection is the enormous portrait of William Thomson (1833–1907), MD, FCPP, a pioneering eye surgeon and one of the first to use an ophthalmoscope and to correct nearsightedness. The portrait's painter, Thomas Eakins (1844–1916), is one of the greatest artists in the history of the United States.

Samuel Emlen (1789–1828), MD, FCPP, acted as physician to a variety of asylums and almshouses in the Philadelphia area. He documented the region's yellow fever epidemic of 1820 and actively campaigned for temperance as a public health measure. This study of Emlen was painted by Thomas Sully (1783–1872), who produced over 2,000 portraits of important social and political celebrities in cities along the East Coast of the United States.

Arthur Vincent Meigs (1850–1912), MD, FCPP, performed research into blood circulation that demonstrated for the first time the structure and function of capillaries. This portrait was painted by William Merritt Chase (1849–1916), who taught at many of the finest art schools in the United States and produced many of the most admired portraits of the 19th century.

Geographer Friedrich Wilhelm Heinrich Alexander von Humboldt (1769–1859) met with Thomas Jefferson in 1804 in order to provide the president with the world's best geographical data on the boundaries of the Spanish possessions in the New World—data that Jefferson put to immediate use in his negotiations with Spain on the boundaries of the Louisiana Purchase. This image of Humboldt was painted by Charles Willson Peale (1741–1827).

George McClellan (1849–1913), MD, FCPP, studied in Vienna under the master anatomist Josef Hyrtl, whose important collection of annotated skulls in the Mütter Museum is one of the world's most significant displays of Hyrtl's work. McClellan became one of the foremost anatomists in the United States. The painter of this portrait, Julian Story (1857–1919), studied and exhibited in Paris, London, Berlin, New York, and Philadelphia.

George Isaac Blumstein (1904–1989), MD, FCPP, served as president of The College of Physicians of Philadelphia from 1970 to 1972. He was given the Distinguished Service Award of the American Academy of Allergy in 1970 and was honored by the Pennsylvania Medical Society in 1979 for 50 years of medical service. This painting was created by Neil Kosh (1926–2010), an award-winning artist who produced, among much other work, 150 commissioned portraits.

Hobart Amory Hare (1862–1931), MD, FCPP, earned an international reputation for his expertise in the diseases of children. After his service as a naval commander during World War I, he served as the president of The College of Physicians of Philadelphia during 1925–1928. This portrait was painted by his daughter Mary Amory Hare (1885–1963), a professional novelist, poet, and playwright.

Robert Tait McKenzie (1867–1938), MD, FCPP, was equally renowned for his accomplishments in medicine, physical education, and sculpture. He made models to illustrate the anatomical expressions of bodily processes, such as fatigue. During World War I, he worked in physical therapy and plastic surgery. He created war memorials that still stand in London, Edinburgh, Ottawa, and Washington, DC. This pastel drawing of McKenzie is one of two created by Violet Oakley (1874–1961), known best for her 43 monumental murals in the capitol of the Commonwealth of Pennsylvania.

Katharine R. Boucot Sturgis (1903–1987), MD, FCPP, was president of The College of Physicians of Philadelphia during 1972–1973. An expert in diseases of the thorax, she was one of the first physicians to perceive the cause-effect relationship between tobacco smoke and lung cancer. This portrait of Sturgis was painted by William Arthur Smith (1918–1966), whose work is represented in the Metropolitan Museum of Art and the National Portrait Gallery.

Roland Gideon Curtin (1839–1913), MD, FCPP, served on medical committees for the Centennial Exposition and International Medical Congress in Philadelphia (1876); the International Congress in Washington, DC (1887); and the World's Congress at the Chicago Exposition (1893). The artist who painted this portrait, William Thomas Smedley (1858–1920), exhibited widely in New York, Philadelphia, and Paris, winning many prizes, awards, and medals.

George Edmund de Schweinitz (1858–1938), MD, FCPP, received many awards for his work as physician, surgeon, lecturer, and clinical professor. His best-known contribution to medical literature is *Diseases of the Eye* (1892), a comprehensive handbook of ophthalmic practices that went through 10 editions. This engaging portrait of Schweinitz was painted by Julian Story, who also painted the portrait of McClellan.

George William Norris (1875–1965), MD, FCPP, represented the third generation of his family to make a career of medicine and to belong to The College of Physicians of Philadelphia. This unusual pastel drawing of Norris by Lazar Raditz (1887–1958) contrasts the beautifully detailed head with a flat, graphic rendering of the body and background.

115

William Potts Dewees (1768–1841), MD, FCPP, was one of the first male obstetricians in the United States. He also offered private instruction on obstetrics to other physicians until that subject was incorporated into the medical curriculum in 1810. This portrait of Dewees is by John Neagle (1796–1865), a painter much influenced by the great artists Thomas Sully (his father-in-law) and Gilbert Stuart.

Nathan Francis Mossell (1856–1946), MD, FCPP, established the Frederick Douglass Memorial Hospital and Training School for Nurses in 1895, which treated many of the wounded soldiers and sailors of the Spanish-American War. The artist, Laura Wheeler Waring (1887–1948), studied at the Pennsylvania Academy of the Fine Arts in Philadelphia and at the Académie de la Grande Chaumière in Paris.

116

Alfred Stillé (1813–1900), MD, FCPP, used his observations of typhus patients during Philadelphia's 1836 epidemic to educate American and European physicians about the distinction between typhus and typhoid fever. (Typhus is spread by lice and fleas; typhoid fever is spread by food contaminated with fecal bacteria.) He was also instrumental in publicly encouraging women to apply to medical school and in encouraging his male colleagues to welcome women into their professional ranks: "So far as I am personally concerned, I not only have no objection to seeing ladies among a medical audience, but, on the other hand, I welcome them." This portrait of Stillé was created by Bernard Uhle (1847–1930), who followed a successful career as a painter with a second career as a photographer. Uhle's presentation of Stillé shows a calm, patient facial expression contradicted by the energetic, nervous hands.

Thomas Cooper (1759–1839), MD, FCPP, an English political activist educated at Oxford University, immigrated to Pennsylvania in 1794 to settle near his friend Joseph Priestley, the discoverer of oxygen. A chemist and mineralogist in addition to being a physician, Cooper brought to his medical practice an unusual breadth of scientific understanding. This portrait is by Charles Willson Peale, who also painted the portrait of Humboldt.

John Hooker Packard (1832–1907), MD, FCPP, was a surgeon during the Civil War, serving in Philadelphia, New Jersey, and Gettysburg. His many contributions to medical literature concern anesthesia, amputation, and tying off blood vessels. The artist, Hugh Henry Breckinridge (1870–1937), was for 50 years associated with the Pennsylvania Academy of Fine Arts, the first art school in the United States.

Louis Adolphus Duhring (1845–1913), MD, FCPP, practiced, taught, and published widely on the diagnosis and treatment of skin diseases. A millionaire upon his death, he bequeathed one-sixth of his fortune to the Historical Medical Library of The College of Physicians of Philadelphia. Hugh Henry Breckenridge (1870–1937), the painter of this portrait, here shows Duhring late in life.

Joseph Price (1853–1911), MD, FCPP, was a pioneer in gynecological surgery. One of the first physicians to emphasize the importance of antiseptic procedures, Price was largely responsible for transforming the hysterectomy from a near-death sentence to a relatively safe surgical operation. This plaster portrait bust of Price was created by Charles Grafley (1862–1929), a winner of dozens of international prizes for his monumental sculptures and portrait busts.

One of the treasures owned by The College of Physicians of Philadelphia is a model of a tartrate crystal created by Louis Pasteur (1822–1995), one of the world's foremost chemists and microbiologists. Pasteur used this model to demonstrate the growth of microorganisms. Until Pasteur proved otherwise, most educated people believed that disease was caused by "bad air," a belief popularized by Aristotle more than 2,000 years earlier.

Other treasures owned by the college include the gold pocket watch and a silver shoe buckle used by Benjamin Rush, MD, FCPP. One of Rush's many contributions to medical history was his provision of the Lewis and Clark Expedition with laxatives containing a high mercury content. The persistence of the mercury in the soil has enabled archeologists to trace the expedition's actual route to the Pacific.

In 1921, physicist Marie Curie (1867–1934) visited The College of Physicians of Philadelphia in order to donate an instrument invented by her husband, Pierre. The Curie piezoelectric generator was the first instrument to determine the energy of electron discharge from radium. Between them, the two Curies won three Nobel Prizes for their pioneering work with radiation—work that revolutionized the practice of medicine.

Joseph Lister
aged about 40

Another treasure of the college includes a small case of surgical instruments and a rack of test tubes used by Sir Joseph Lister (1827–1912), a pioneer of antiseptic surgery. Lister used carbolic acid to sanitize surgical instruments, incisions, and dressings, thereby greatly reducing the incidence of infections in his patients.

Jacob da Silva Solis-Cohen (1838–1927), MD, FCPP, was awarded a Congressional Medal of Honor for his service during the Civil War. The first physician to organize and deliver systematic training on laryngology to medical students in the United States, he founded and coedited the first medical journal on the subject. He also performed the world's first successful laryngotomy for cancer of a vocal cord. This portrait of Solis-Cohen was painted by William Taylor Thomson (1858–1941), a well-known Philadelphia artist who, in addition to creating this unusual portrait and many others, contributed illustrations to numerous books and periodicals. Pictured at 89 years old shortly before his death, Solis-Cohen is shown in the traditional pose of a philosopher deep in thought. Thomson's brushwork, however, displays a freedom of movement that is quite modern.

Nine

INTO THE FUTURE

The Karabots Junior Fellows Program provides practical assistance, mentoring, and academic support to Philadelphia high school students from communities underrepresented in health care professions. Athena and Nicholas Karabots, shown here with junior fellow Najee Warlow, provided the initial funding for the program. The "Karabots Kids" reach out to their peers on health issues through public service videos posted to the college's social media.

Smallpox, polio, and diphtheria are just three of the diseases that killed or permanently injured millions of people before vaccination brought them under control. The college presents the fascinating stories of these and other vaccine-preventable diseases through its award-winning History of Vaccines website, with media-rich timelines, activities, articles, interviews with researchers, and content from the college's Historical Medical Library.

The college's annual fundraiser, the Mütter Ball, celebrates the birthday of Thomas Dent Mütter, MD, FCPP, and attracts fans of the Mütter Museum from all over the United States. Costumes abound, with some devotees even dressing as favorite museum specimens. The absinthe lounge, celebrity disc jockeys, and anatomically themed hors d'oeuvres are always great hits with the party crowd.

The college is booked most days and nights of the year for private fundraiser galas, corporate events, filming and photography, and personal celebrations. With its many elegant interconnecting rooms, fragrant herb garden, and edgy Mütter Museum to stimulate conversation, the college has become a popular destination for those wishing to marry or otherwise celebrate in a beautiful and unique environment.

The Mütter Museum Store, like the museum itself, houses a fascinating collection of objects. Giant fluffy microbes, ether perfume labeled with the exclusive umlaut logo (*ü*), handcrafted dolls in the form of conjoined twins, and the famous Mütter Museum art books and calendars tempt every visitor to leave lighter in the wallet and in the heart, knowing that proceeds from purchases benefit the museum.

BIBLIOGRAPHY

Bell, Whitfield J. *The College of Physicians of Philadelphia: A Bicentennial History*. Canton, MA: Science History Publications, 1987.

Berkowitz, Julie S. *The College of Physicians of Philadelphia Portrait Catalogue*. Philadelphia: The College of Physicians of Philadelphia, 1984.

Fenn, Elizabeth A. *Pox Americana: The Great Smallpox Epidemic of 1775–82*. New York: Hill and Wang, 2001.

Lindgren, Laura, ed. *Mütter Museum Historic Medical Photographs*. New York: Blast, 2007.

Marion, John Francis. *Philadelphia Medica: Being a Guide to the City's Historical Places of Health Interest*. Harisburg, PA: SmithKline, 1975.

Worden, Gretchen. *Mütter Museum of The College of Physicians of Philadelphia*. New York: Blast, 2002.

ABOUT THE COLLEGE OF PHYSICIANS OF PHILADELPHIA

The College of Physicians of Philadelphia is the oldest professional medical organization in the United States, founded by 24 physicians in 1787 "to advance the science of medicine and to thereby lessen human misery." Today, over 1,500 fellows (elected members) continue to convene at the college and to work toward better serving the public. Throughout its history, the college has provided a place for medical professionals and the general public to learn about medicine as both a science and an art. This historic spirit continues in the current mission of the college: advancing the cause of health while upholding the ideals and heritage of medicine. The college strives to enable individuals, families, and communities to take greater responsibility for their health; to improve the health of the public through service to health professionals; to enhance appreciation of the heritage of medicine; and to provide information for the development of health policy. The college is home to the Mütter Museum and the Historical Medical Library. Its outreach programs include phillyhealthinfo.org (an online health information, resource, and educational program serving the Delaware Valley) and the C. Everett Koop Community Education Center. The public is invited to attend the many lectures, workshops, and conferences offered by the college. These programs reflect the college's reverence for the past, its commitment to the present, and its vision for the future of medicine and health.

Your support helps the college explore the history and the future of health care and promote public understanding of contemporary health care issues. Sales of this book benefit the college and all its programs.

The College of Physicians of Philadelphia
19 South Twenty-second Street
Philadelphia, PA 19103-3097
Phone: 215-563-3737
www.collegeofphysicians.org

Visit us at
arcadiapublishing.com

www.ingramcontent.com/pod-product-compliance
Lightning Source LLC
Chambersburg PA
CBHW080614110426

42813CB00006B/1505